The Distance Between

OTHER BOOKS BY MIKE MCINTYRE

NONFICTION

The Kindness of Strangers: Penniless Across America

The Wander Year: One Couple's Journey Around the World

FICTION

The Scavenger's Daughter: A Tyler West Mystery

The Distance Between:

A Travel Memoir

MIKE MCINTYRE

Copyright © 2013 by Mike McIntyre.

All rights reserved. No part of this book may be reproduced, uploaded to the Internet, or copied without permission of the author, except by a reviewer, who may quote brief passages in a review.

To get an email alert when Mike McIntyre's next book is released, sign up here: http://eepurl.com/Jl_gn

ISBN-13: 978-1494421168
ISBN-10: 149442116X

CONTENTS

A Note to Readers i
PROLOGUE: Crossing the Line 1
ESCAPES 3
    As Quick as You Like 5
    The Teacher 16
    You Alright? 23
    Time 30
    Disneyland 34
    First Day in Antigua, Guatemala 38
    Which Way? 41
CUSTOMS 57
    Bhutan's National Sport 59
    A Saudi Super Bowl 61
    Wrestling My Conscience 63
    Day of the Dead 70
    Sundays in Budapest 72
    The Chicken in the Church 77
    A Cross Between Mardi Gras and Arson 79
    Halloween at World's End 82
    Machetes 87
    The Aduana 88
    Hanging in Paris 92

CONFLICTS ... 95
- Extreme Skiing ... 97
- Wishes ... 102
- Smiles ... 106
- Live and Let Live ... 114
- Boom-Boom ... 121
- The Birthday Party ... 132
- Rambo in Yuma ... 136

TRANSITS ... 139
- Final Approach ... 141
- First Flight ... 143
- Widespread Panic ... 147
- Tsunami Train ... 150
- No Man's Land ... 154
- Passengers ... 156
- All Aboard! ... 159
- Africa ... 161

ENCOUNTERS ... 169
- The Gringo's Shoes ... 171
- One Day ... 175
- Needs ... 178
- Sexy Beast ... 185
- A Good Life ... 190
- The Amazing Dr. X ... 193
- Marriage and Chinese Food ... 196
- The Villa Delfina ... 198
- Transitions ... 205
- Sad but True ... 210

Details	216
Strays	219
Thank You	223
About the Author	225
Also by Mike McIntyre	227

A NOTE TO READERS

The following stories take place between 1965 and 2013. Some of the names have been changed. The rest is as I remember it.

PROLOGUE: CROSSING THE LINE

The first border I crossed was the state line between California and Nevada. I was eight. My family had recently moved from Sacramento up to Lake Tahoe, which straddles the two states. We lived on the California side. I drew crayon maps of my new home, with the lake bisected by the state line. When I couldn't stand it anymore, I begged my parents to show me the real thing.

My dad, mom, little brother and I piled into the station wagon and drove to Crystal Bay, at the top of the north shore. It was a school night. Lady Bug, our Old English sheepdog, came too. Some relation of hers had appeared in the movies *The Shaggy Dog* and *Please Don't Eat the Daisies*. In my mind, she was a celebrity. She was born at a kennel in Colorado and had already crossed three state lines. Was I jealous? You bet.

I spotted the sign for Cal-Neva, a lodge and casino once owned by Frank Sinatra. His guests had included Rat Pack pals Dean Martin, Sammy Davis Jr., and Peter Lawford, as well as John F. Kennedy. Marilyn Monroe had stayed in one of the cabins the weekend before she died. When authorities discovered Chicago mobster Sam Giancana had a piece of the casino, they yanked Sinatra's gaming license.

Part of the Cal-Neva resort stood in California, and the other part in Nevada. The state line was painted on the bottom of the hotel swimming pool. It was also embedded in the carpet of the casino floor. I'd see these things many years later, but not on this night. You had to be twenty-one to go inside.

My dad parked the car on Highway 28, just shy of the Crystal Bay Club, another casino. I got out. The casino was painted a garish green and bathed in neon. I peered through a giant plate-glass window. Women who left smeared lipstick on their cocktail glasses—highballs, they called them—fed nickels into a row of slot machines. Their husbands wore hats and smoked unfiltered cigarettes. It was an exotic scene, but nothing like the nearby sign—the one that said: "Welcome to Nevada."

I sprinted toward the sign. When I crossed over that great, invisible line, I felt my life change.

That's what did it for me. That's what started the itch.

My dad called to me from the station wagon.

"Mikey boy!"

I returned to California that night, never imagining all the lines I would cross to get where I was going.

ESCAPES

"Why do you wonder that globe-trotting does not help you, seeing that you always take yourself with you? The reason that set you wandering is ever at your heels."

—Socrates

AS QUICK AS YOU LIKE

I loved the cocktail waitress and she loved me, but she loved her husband more. I had three days off from the restaurant where we worked in Lake Tahoe. I needed some distance. I also needed to be around some people with bigger problems. So I booked a red-eye to New York.

Tahoe was headed for a record snowfall that year—a thousand inches, as I recall. I ditched my VW Beetle in a snowbank in Truckee and rode a Greyhound over Donner Summit. At the Sacramento bus station, waiting for the airport shuttle, I dropped a quarter into one of the pay TVs. There was only snow.

It was midnight. A woman with rumpled clothes and stringy hair whimpered into a payphone, a busted suitcase at her feet.

"Please," she said, "please."

She listened to the reply on the other end.

"Don't hang up!" she screamed. "DON'T HANG UP! DON'T—"

She set the phone in the cradle and collapsed down the wall to the floor. Her chest heaved as she bawled.

"Oh, God, nooooo. Oh, God, nooooo. Oh, God…"

I realized I'd momentarily forgotten my own heartache. I glanced around the bus station. Everybody looked sad. I wondered if I should just hang out there for the next three days.

After landing at LaGuardia the next morning, I checked into the Sloan House YMCA, on West 34th Street. It was my third stay there. The place was a genuine downer, a giant version of the Sacramento bus station. It was perfect.

Sophie's Choice had recently opened in theaters and I bought a ticket. People in the seats around me wept when Sophie told Stingo how the Nazis forced her to choose which of her two children would live, and again when Sophie and Nathan committed suicide.

But I wasn't distracted by Sophie's woes. I couldn't get the cocktail waitress out of my mind.

Maybe I hadn't traveled far enough.

I spotted an ad in the *New York Times* for ninety-nine-dollar day trips to the Bahamas. The travel agent said I needed a passport, birth certificate or voter registration card to enter the country. I hadn't brought my passport to New York—and who carries around his birth certificate or voter registration card?

Times Square was still a seedy district of porno joints, hookers, pimps and drug peddlers. It was also the place to score a fake ID. I ducked into a cubbyhole of a shop and asked the man behind the counter if they made birth certificates.

"Yeah, we make birth certificates," he said.

I already knew that. I'd seen the samples in the window. But none of them looked good enough to fool Bahamian immigration. I didn't see any samples of what I really wanted.

"Well?" the man said.

He was big and bald and he chomped on a cigar.

"Um, can you make me a voter registration card?" I mumbled.

"What?"

I repeated the question.

The man shook his head. He turned to another man he'd been talking to.

"See what I mean? All these guys come in here, they never want the first thing they ask for. It's always the second."

He turned back to me. "No, I can't make you a voter registration card, asshole—it's against the law! Now get the fuck outta here!"

He jabbed his cigar at the door.

I was halfway down the block when it occurred to me I didn't need a *fake* voter registration card.

I stopped at a payphone and dialed the number for the New York City Board of Elections.

A clerk said she could mail me a voter registration form.

When I asked how I could get my card that day, she told me I'd need to apply in person at the main office.

I popped out of the subway in Lower Manhattan and asked an elderly woman for directions. She insisted on escorting me to the Board of Elections building. She stopped and pointed her umbrella at a spot across the Hudson River.

"That's where Aaron Burr and Alexander Hamilton had their famous duel," she said.

I wondered how many people got a U.S. history lesson on their way to committing fraud.

When I registered to vote, my hand shook as I filled out the form.

In the box for "address," I wrote down the street number for the YMCA.

A clerk reviewed the form.

"Apartment number?" he said.

I hesitated, then gave him the number of my room at the Y.

"Sign here."

I signed below the sentence that began, "I declare under penalty of perjury…"

The clerk congratulated me as he handed me my voter registration card and said I should feel proud for fulfilling my civic duty.

The plane departed Newark for the Bahamas at six the next morning. The itinerary was three hours down, five hours on the ground and three hours back.

A bus shuttled passengers from the Nassau airport to a hotel-casino on the beach.

I'd packed for wintry New York, so I sweated as I trudged along the hot sand in my pants and long-sleeve shirt.

I took a stool at a beach shack called the Arawak Bar and told the bartender to make me his specialty. He mixed me a Yellow Bird, one of those sweet tropical drinks that sneak up on you. He made me another, then a few more. I was hammered when the casino opened at noon.

I had eighty-five dollars. My pleasure was poker, but there were no games.

I sat down at a blackjack table. My stake was gone before the dealer reshuffled.

I was three thousand miles from home and busted.

The casino would cash a personal check for up to two hundred dollars. I wrote one for the max, knowing I had only eleven dollars in my checking account. I'd use the two hundred to win back the eighty-five, then return the two hundred to the cashier in exchange for my check.

I went back to the blackjack table and played four hands simultaneously for fifty dollars each.

The dealer showed a six, a likely bust card.

I stood pat on all four hands, two of which totaled twenty.

I pictured my stack doubling and vowed to cash out and leave the casino.

The dealer revealed his hole card, a ten, then drew a five for a twenty-one.

"Thanks for playing," he said, taking my chips.

My knees buckled as I stepped back from the table.

I now had a bad check to cover, plus I had no money to get from Newark to LaGuardia for my red-eye back to California—not to mention the bus fare from Sacramento to my car in Truckee.

I recalled I could cash a check with my American Express card.

Trouble was, the local AMEX office was miles away in downtown Nassau, and the return shuttle to the airport left in less than an hour.

I climbed into a taxi in front of the casino. I didn't tell the cabbie I was penniless.

We crossed the bridge and got stuck in traffic. Traffic cops in white uniforms and pith helmets waved their arms as we inched along.

I worried I might miss my flight back to the U.S.—or worse, make the flight but not have enough time to cover my losses.

When I sensed we were almost to the American Express office, the cabbie stopped for gas.

"Please, I'm in a hurry," I said.

The cabbie rushed to the pump, where an attendant met him.

"Five dollars," the cabbie said, "as quick as you like."

The singsongy expression lingered in the air, and for an instant everything changed.

I was no longer a lovelorn fool in the midst of a rum-fueled gambling binge. Instead I was a traveler, gripped by some native vernacular.

But the moment soon passed and the fever returned.

I traded a rubber check for five hundred dollars in American Express traveler's checks.

Back at the casino, I exchanged those for five hundred dollars in chips. The cabbie had followed me to the cashier's window. I broke a fifty-dollar chip and paid him his fare, stuffing the remaining twenty bucks in my pocket.

I had ten minutes until my shuttle to the airport.

I rushed across the casino floor toward the blackjack table, then changed course when I heard the commotion at the craps table.

"Come on, baby!"

"Come on, seven!"

"Come on, shooter!"

I elbowed my way in and set my chips on the rail.

A freckled man in a tropical shirt held the dice. Towers of chips were stacked in front of him, and he was whooping it up good.

He was due for a reversal of fortune.

I placed a hundred dollars in chips on the "Don't Pass" bar and bet against the freckled man.

"Coming out," the stickman barked.

The freckled man shook the dice and let them fly.

"Seven a winner," the stickman said. "Winner seven."

The freckled man and the other bettors erupted in cheers. The dealer paid off their bets and dragged mine away.

I doubled down, placing another two hundred dollars on the "Don't Pass" bar.

The freckled man blew on the dice and tossed them, and they bounced off the back wall of the table.

"Eleven," the stickman said. "Eleven a winner."

More cheers.

"You should get a piece of this," the freckled man told me, stacking his chips.

I set my last one hundred fifty dollars in chips on the table. Only this time I placed the chips on the "Pass" line. The freckled man saw this and switched his bet to the "Don't Pass" bar. The other bettors followed suit. Clearly, I was bad luck.

The freckled man rolled the dice.

Up came the dreaded Ace-Deuce.

"Three, craps," the stickman said. "Line away, pay the Don'ts."

The dealer snatched up my chips and paid the others. The freckled man cashed out.

I pulled my last twenty from my pocket. The stickman pushed the dice to me with his stick.

"New shooter," he said.

The dealer asked if I wanted chips. I studied the casino entrance, where the airport shuttle would soon be departing. The stickman rapped the table with his stick.

"Pick 'em up, shooter."

I stuffed the twenty in my pocket and headed for the door.

I managed to get back to Lake Tahoe the following afternoon. I went to work early to set up the bar. The balcony facing the lake was heaped with fresh snow. A bald eagle landed on the railing. I'd never seen one. It looked so beautiful and majestic. It looked like it knew where it was going. It made me feel even worse.

The cocktail waitress arrived and I acted busy. She came up to the bar, all smiles. I was so mad at her but I couldn't keep from smiling back.

She said she had something to tell me.

I followed her through the kitchen and out the employee entrance. She pulled me into the freight elevator, and when the doors closed she kissed me. She'd had a change of heart, she said. I kissed her back. We reached the ground floor. The doors opened and closed. We held each other tight. I didn't tell her where I'd been or what I'd done. My credit rating would be shot and bill collectors would hound me. But at that moment, holding the cocktail waitress in my arms and riding that freight elevator up and down, up and down, it all seemed worth it.

A couple weeks later I shaved my head, and the cocktail waitress freaked out and moved home to Minnesota.

I waited a couple months and sent her a card, beseeching her to return. I taped a lock of a buddy's blond hair to the card and wrote, "It's growing in fast!" She drove back to California and forgave me even though I was still bald as a baby. Things were swell and then they weren't. She finally left me for her husband, who had a beautiful head of hair.

About a year later, I sat down at a seven-card stud table at the Harrah's in Reno. I won a few pots and was up more than seven hundred dollars, about what I had lost in the Bahamas. If that fact registered with me, I didn't dwell on it. I instead sat at the same table for three days without sleep, gambling away my winnings, my original stake and a few credit card cash advances. I staggered out onto Virginia Street just after sunrise, and the adrenaline that had sustained me through my poker marathon seeped out of my body. I feared I might topple into traffic. I was too spent to drive back to the lake, and I had no money for a room.

I had heard that the cocktail waitress was now divorced and living in Reno, attending college. I didn't want her to see me this way, but there was nobody else to call. I found her number in the phone book.

She picked me up on the corner and drove me to her apartment. We didn't talk much. I crashed on her bed while she studied in the living room. I slept all day and through the night. In the morning, she drove me back to the casino to get my car. I didn't have money to tip the valet. I asked the cocktail waitress if she could loan me a dollar. She offered me more. I said just the one would do.

That night, after closing the bar, I pulled a dollar from my tip jar and mailed it to the cocktail waitress. For a long time, it was the only debt I was able to repay. A few months later I moved to Washington, D.C., and my life started over.

That was more than thirty years ago. Along the way I learned a truth about travel: we will take a trip for one reason but remember it for another. Until I sat down to write this story, I'd given little thought over the decades to the cocktail waitress who sent me careening off to New York and the Bahamas. Instead, my enduring impression from that seventy-two-hour misadventure is something I dismissed at the time: the cabbie, and his lilting lingo.

As quick as you like. I love that expression. Through the years I've made it my own. Hardly a week passes that I don't utter it. Usually to my wife, Andrea. I'll tack it onto a request to soften the tone. But most of the time it's just a joke, something I like to say. Sometimes I'll deliver it with a Caribbean accent. Andrea always replies, "This *is* as quick as I like." I've never told her the circumstances of how I came by it.

I eventually realized the cabbie's expression, while a mere throwaway, was something authentic. It offered a fleeting glimpse into a life different from mine, a way of viewing the day from another angle.

The world is shrinking. It's become harder to journey anywhere and be surprised. Returning home with a little nugget like, "as quick as you like," is as good a reward of travel as any.

I had never heard the expression, "as quick as you like," until that day in the Nassau gas station. I've never heard it since. Sometimes I wonder if the cabbie coined it. And sometimes I wonder if I simply misunderstood.

THE TEACHER

I was twenty, waiting to turn twenty-one, when I'd receive my visa to work in Saudi Arabia. I decided to wait on the beach in Mexico and flew to Puerto Vallarta. I had a wispy mustache, as blond as the sand. It didn't look bad when I leaned in close to the bathroom mirror. What did I know?

A water taxi dropped me for the day in Mismaloya, a secluded village down the coast. A few seafood shacks flanked one end of the beach. On a hillside above the cove stood the Night of the Iguana Bar & Grill, named for the Richard Burton movie that was filmed there. The curve of sand faced green sea rocks that jutted from the blue Pacific. The place was still years from the grasp of high-rise condos and resorts.

A lone woman was reading on the beach when I stepped off the boat. I spread my towel in the sand a respectable distance from her and opened a book. When we looked up from our books at the same time, she smiled and waved me over.

She was from Connecticut, where she taught elementary school. It was her summer vacation. I'd always been interested in girls, but this teacher was a real woman. She had a woman's name and a woman's beach tote bag and a woman's bathing suit—a one-piece that stirred my imagination. We talked for hours. I studied her sensual lips and her adorable Ali

MacGraw-like overlapping front tooth. Before she returned to town, she asked me to join her for dinner, seven o'clock.

Everything I brought to Mexico fit in a daypack. I thought traveling light would feel liberating, but now that I had a date with an older woman it only felt idiotic. Aside from the swimsuit and T-shirt I wore to the beach, my only other clothes were a pink, pinstriped shirt and a pair of crotch-hugging Ocean Pacific corduroy shorts—both dirty.

I hustled to the *lavandería* and stood in my bathing suit, watching my two articles of clothing wash and dry in the coin-operated machines. I borrowed an iron and ironing board from the owner and ironed every wrinkle from the shirt. There wasn't much I could do for the shorts.

When I returned to my posada to dress for dinner, I realized I'd lost my wallet. My swimsuit had no pockets, so I had set my wallet on a table at the lavandería while I ironed my clothes. I ran back to the lavandería but my wallet was gone. The owner hadn't seen it, she said. I checked at the local police station in case someone had turned it in. No luck. The wallet contained all my cash, a credit card, a bankcard and a fake ID that showed me to be twenty-three rather than twenty.

My passport and traveler's checks were in my room. But the posada wasn't equipped to cash my traveler's checks, and the banks were closed. I was already late for dinner, but I didn't want to turn up unable to pay the bill. A *casa de cambio* was open, the posada owner said, but it was in the opposite direction from the teacher's hotel. Sweat poured from me as I dashed through the streets of Puerto Vallarta. By the time I exchanged my traveler's checks for pesos and reached the teacher's hotel, I was ninety minutes late.

I was surprised to find her still waiting for me in the hotel restaurant. She sat alone at a table, facing the entrance. A mariachi band played. She looked expectantly at me as I crossed the room. She wore an aqua-colored sundress, red lipstick and gold earrings. She had not yet ordered and had barely touched her margarita.

I sat down and explained why I was so late.

"I knew something must have happened, that's why I waited," she said. "I just knew you weren't that type of guy."

Although I'd often behave like one in the future, I was still too young and inexperienced to understand what she meant by "that type of guy."

We spent much of the next week together. During the day we'd go snorkeling and read on the beach. At night we'd cross the footbridge into the heart of town and eat at one of the restaurants along the Paseo Diaz Ordaz, stopping near the seawall to watch the sunset. I'd walk her to the gate of her boutique hotel every evening, then return to my little room at the posada.

One night, before crossing the bridge back over the Rio Cuale, we saw some children playing soccer on a cement playground below the street level. I descended the steps and kicked the semi-flat ball with the kids. Several boys sidled up to measure their height against mine. Their eyes grew comically big as they stared up at me. I saw the teacher watching and wondered what she thought of this tall, skinny American fellow playing soccer with a troop of Mexican kids. I knew what I wanted but hesitated to act. I wasn't yet sure what the teacher wanted.

On her last night in Puerto Vallarta, the teacher and I again ate dinner in her hotel restaurant. She wrote her name, address and phone number on a cocktail napkin and passed it to me. I studied the teacher's cursive handwriting and got the chills. I folded the napkin in four and put it in my pocket. When she asked if I wanted to see her room, I gulped and said yes.

We stood on her balcony, transfixed by a lightning storm over the nearby mountains. When the rain arrived and pelted us we rushed inside. The teacher offered me a towel and I dried my face and neck and arms. She took the towel from me and I wondered what came next.

The teacher pulled something from a plastic bag. It was one of those festive Mexican wedding shirts, with flowers embroidered on the front and the cuffs. She had obviously grown tired of seeing me in the same shirt every day.

She walked toward me with the shirt.

"Turn around," she said. "I want to see if this fits."

She held the shirt up to my back and smoothed the top of it across my shoulders. She ran a hand down the right sleeve, pressing it against my arm. When she reached the bottom she held the cuff against my wrist.

I'd never felt anything so erotic.

"Perfect," she said.

I was ready to turn around and take her in my arms when she added, "You're the same size as my Mike."

The teacher had a fiancé, and he shared my name. He'd wear the Mexican shirt later that summer when they got married on a beach in Connecticut.

I was grateful my back was still turned; it gave me time to lose the stunned look on my face.

The teacher folded the shirt and returned it to the bag. She said she had to catch an early bus for Guadalajara in the morning, and did I want to meet for breakfast?

The next day, after breakfast, I carried the teacher's suitcase as we walked to the bus station. Before she boarded she gave me a peck on the cheek.

The whole episode stung for only a short while. I was young and fortunate and excited about my impending move to Saudi Arabia. There was no reason to feel sad.

I flew back to the States and bought a new wallet. I tucked the napkin with the teacher's details into the wallet, in a pocket under the credit card slots. I don't even know why.

When I returned home from Saudi Arabia the following year, I got a new, smaller wallet. While transferring contents from the old wallet to the new one, I came across the folded cocktail napkin. I hadn't seen it since I'd left the Middle East. I unfolded it and read the teacher's name and address and phone number. I had no reason to keep it, but I did.

I never liked the feel of a wallet, the bulk of it in my hip pocket. It was uncomfortable to sit on. So over the years, I kept buying smaller and slimmer wallets, and I'd pare down their contents. But I always found room for the teacher's napkin. I could've transferred the information to a scrap of paper. It would've saved a lot of space. But I moved the napkin from wallet to wallet, even as it began to fall apart.

When I became a full-time traveler in my mid-thirties, I grew wary of pickpockets and I pitched my last wallet. I instead carried my money in my right front pocket and my driver's license and credit cards in my left. I didn't have room for a crumbling cocktail napkin. So I discarded it.

Five years after I met the teacher, I returned to Puerto Vallarta on a whim. I walked the streets, searching for a vacant room. I recognized the hotel where the teacher had stayed and I inquired at the front desk. Before the clerk passed me the key, I knew it would fit the lock to the teacher's old room.

Her room looked exactly as it had five years ago. And as I stood in the middle of it, I could almost feel the teacher smoothing that shirt flat across my shoulders. I stared at the bed and wondered if it was the same one.

I drank too many *cervezas* and awoke around dawn with a hangover. I crossed the bridge to seek some hair of the dog. Nothing was open. The cement playground where I'd played soccer with the kids was cracked and full of weeds. City workers were spraying the seawall with some sort of chemical. I noticed my right hand had swollen to twice the size of my left, and I couldn't stop looking at it.

In the afternoon, a hotel caretaker asked if I'd like to see the view from the roof. He pointed to a small structure at the top of an exterior spiral staircase.

"Coconuts," he said, meaning the adjacent palm trees.

I followed him up the stairs and we arrived at a room resembling a tree house, with views of palms swaying by the sea. There was a crude table, a couple barrel chairs and a cot. It was the caretaker's quarters.

He poured us shot glasses of cheap white tequila from a gallon-sized plastic bottle. I tossed mine back and he poured me another. I gazed at the Pacific and felt the caretaker rubbing my shoulders. As I flinched, his hands hurried down my chest and plunged inside my shorts. His tequila breath was hot against my neck. I threw him off and vaulted down the stairs three at a time.

In my room, I pulled the napkin from my wallet and reached for the phone on the nightstand. "Hey, you'll never guess who this is and where I am," I imagined saying. But I didn't dial the number. I packed my bag and took the next bus out of town.

I was twenty-five but already felt fifty. In the period between those two Puerto Vallarta visits, I'd somehow lost my way. My confidence, born of youth and ignorance, was gone. So was nearly all of my hope. I was by turns despondent, cynical, paranoid and numb. And for the longest time, there wasn't anyone who could teach me anything.

YOU ALRIGHT?

Everyone in Nacogdoches, Texas, asked me, "You alright?" I knew it was their way of saying howdy, but I took them literally and always replied, "Yeah, I'm alright." But it was a lie.

Earlier that week I got gutted in a Las Vegas poker room. I was in town for the Grateful Dead's three-day run at the Silver Bowl. In between shows, I kept returning to the ten-twenty stud table at the Mirage until I'd lost all the money I'd planned to live on for the next year. Almost all of it, anyway. I was down to my last six hundred bucks. If I could get back to Guatemala, I could live on ten dollars a day. Even so, the idea of looking for work in sixty days instead of a year distressed me. The woman I wanted didn't want me, and the woman who wanted me told me not to call if I couldn't call regularly. Vegas is no place to feel lost. I couldn't even make it through the last concert. A few Deadheads sprayed the overheated crowd with water bottles rumored to be laced with acid. I panicked and headed for the Bummer Tent. But when Jerry launched into "He's Gone," I took it as a sign and bolted. I found my car on the Boulder Highway and aimed it toward Texas.

This was when I was still a half-hearted drifter. I needed to be reassured that there was still a place for me in the "real" world, so I'd migrate between the foreign and the familiar. I kept repeating the same circuit, usually by car: Guatemala, Mexico, New Orleans, Vegas, Lake Tahoe. Sometimes I'd travel alone, sometimes with other vagabonds. A couple times we detoured to Death Valley to toss a Frisbee on the salt flats of Badwater Basin—282 feet below sea level and 120 degrees Fahrenheit. It felt like the thing to do. Now Nacogdoches. Again.

I was driving a blue Buick Century beater I'd picked up in Texas the month before. The wholesaler I bought it from had misplaced the pink slip. He said he'd send it to me, but he never did. I left messages for him from the road that went unreturned. A couple times his wife answered the phone and told me to quit pestering her about some pink slip she knew nothing about. For all I knew, there was no pink slip and the Buick was hot. A few days earlier, when I was still flush, I might have abandoned the car in Vegas. But now I was busted and needed to sell it. I'd paid four hundred dollars for it but figured I could get six. That'd double my time left on the drift. But no pink slip, no sale.

The wholesaler didn't look surprised when I turned up at his clapboard house deep in the woods outside Nacogdoches. He invited me into his office. The dark room was lined with bulging file cabinets, and his desk was heaped with papers. He sat down and casually said, "You was wantin' that pink slip, were you?" I seethed and demanded to know why I had to drive fourteen hundred miles for a piece of paper he should've already mailed to me. The man shifted in his chair in a way that afforded me a good, long gander at the pistol in his waistband. Then he pawed through some papers in the drawer, giving me a glimpse of the other gun in there.

"I'm sure sorry, but I haven't placed my hands on it just yet," he said. "When I do, I'll be sure to let you know."

It was typical Deep East Texas: some fellow basically threatening your life while being all calm and polite about it.

This was my third pass through Nacogdoches in as many weeks. A friend I knocked around with in Central America was from there, and I liked the sound of the name: *Nackuh-dochiz*. Sometimes Dwight called it "Nackuh-nowhcrc," and occasionally "Nackuh—smile when you say it, get down, fireplug—dochiz."

The place had a legend. There was once an Indian chief in the region with two sons, Natchitoches and Nacogdoches. The chief shot an arrow to the east and another to the west and told his sons to find them. Natchitoches picked up the arrow in the east, in what is now Louisiana, and founded the town that bears his name. Nacogdoches followed the arrow to the west and founded the Texas town. Nacogdoches, the town, is also the oldest settlement in Texas, a claim disputed by the citizens of nearby San Augustine.

Everyone I met in Nacogdoches lived in trailers, and everyone they knew lived in trailers. Some folks had two trailers parked side by side in the patchy grass, with rusted barbecues and busted lawn furniture in between. One fellow reclined in his plastic chaise lounge, swigged whisky and shot a BB gun at feral cats. In the late afternoons, Dwight's buddies would come around, guzzle Coors Lights and say, "You alright?"

Every night we'd end up at some sports bar in a strip mall or at a cavernous dance hall at the end of a dirt road out in the pines. There was always a shuffleboard and guys who sprayed tobacco juice as they crowed, "See ya, wouldn't wanna be ya!" after knocking your puck over the edge. When the music started, these boys would eye the ladies on the dance floor and talk of plans to "get a nut off" or "get a leg over."

Dwight wasn't much for line dancing, but he was good with a line. He'd sidle up to a gal with hair and nails out to here and say, "Darlin', love is a pretty harsh word, but I'm fixin' to use it." Dwight loved to make women laugh. They would gather around, and they'd all ask me if I was alright, and I'd grin and lie, lie, lie.

Dwight's trailer didn't have an extra bed. I'd slumber atop a heap of laundry, which only intensified the heat and humidity of those Nacogdoches nights.

After lunch, a group of us would meet for hoops at the court outside the Baptist Rec Center over on Austin Street. The court wasn't level, but I perfected a long-range jump shot, uphill and into the Deep East Texas wind. When I caught myself declaring after every swish, "See ya, wouldn't wanna be ya!" I figured it was time to press on.

Dwight knew cars, and he knew the wholesaler who owed me the pink slip on my Buick. He told me to leave the car with him, and he'd sort out the paperwork and sell it for me. He also owned a little import shop across from the college. I had some leftover Guatemalan *tipica* goods—hand-woven hats and belts and bracelets—I'd been selling at street fairs in Northern California. Dwight said his store would take them on consignment. He'd bring me the money for the car and handicrafts the next time he came shopping in Antigua. I told him I only had enough dough to hold out down there for two months. He told me not to worry; he promised he'd get there in time.

I had a voucher for two hundred dollars on American Airlines. These were the days when you could still write a letter of complaint to an airline and it would issue you travel credit for your "inconvenience." My voucher covered a one-way flight from Dallas to Tegucigalpa, Honduras. Hitchhiking was easy in Honduras, and drivers would often throw a pineapple or mango into the deal. And once inside Guatemala, truckers would give you a lift for a few *quetzales*.

I settled back into Antigua but steered clear of the restaurants and bars where I was known as a big spender and generous tipper. I instead ate cheaply at the hole-in-the-wall *comedores* or at the group tables inside the sprawling *mercado*. Some days I'd get by on a fried tortilla topped with avocado and a sprinkling of cheese, sold from baskets by the Mayan women near the central park. A man on the outskirts of town rented me a cold-water cottage on his property for less than five dollars a day. I stretched my funds as long as I could. But after two months I was tapped out, and I'd never seen nor heard from Dwight. My predicament was entirely my fault, but I still felt like my buddy had let me down.

Antigua had never looked lovelier than it did the day I had to say *adios* to it. The rainy season was over and the sky above the colonial city was now a brilliant blue. I cursed myself as I made my way toward the first in a series of chicken buses that would carry me north. How could I blow a year's worth of travel funds on a poker game? I'd chucked a good journalism job a few months earlier to head out on the road. Now I'd have to crawl back to California and take some crap job at some crap newspaper. I'd left a few things at a friend's in San Diego. I tried to recall whether a necktie was among them. A tie! The thought of wearing one again made me want to hang myself.

That's when Dwight emerged from the crowd. He sported a new buzz cut and one of those floral thrift-store shirts he'd wear for days on end. He had my money. Eight hundred dollars for the car and four hundred for the handicrafts.

Dwight was disappointed when I confessed I'd given up on him and nearly left town.

"I told you I'd be here," he said, forking over twelve one hundred-dollar bills.

The whole time I knew Dwight, he was always handing out money, and I wondered whether he had really sold the Buick. Maybe he was pretending he had and was instead coming to my rescue. I'd watched him befriend shoeless urchins in the park, give them nicknames like Jo-Jo and Elvis, then buy them sneakers and shirts and lunch. He never passed a beggar without giving him at least a few coins. He'd have his hand in his pocket before they even asked. "If I don't give them money, they might not eat that day," he'd explain. Despite this streak of kindness, Dwight would often claim with chilling certitude he was going to hell. He was a good friend—a better friend than me—and I always felt guilty I ever doubted him.

Those cardsharps in Vegas had cut me up good, but my luck had changed. I'd come close a time or two, but I'd never go broke again. Never wear a tie again, either. Things fell into place. I got some good writing done. I met some people I'll never forget. Not everything would work out, but I'd snag more than my share of good fortune. That day in Antigua was when I hit my drifter's stride.

I told Dwight we had to go out and celebrate—on me, of course. We started with the *lomito* and big bowls of the signature *caldo de pollo* at La Fonda de la Calle Real. Then we made the circuit of the nightspots: Mistral, Picasso, La Chimenea. When the bars closed, we were hungry again, so we hit the all-night chicken joint. For once, the dogs didn't bark at me on the walk home.

Maybe it was because we were in Guatemala and not in Texas, but Dwight never asked me the question he and his pals always put to me in Nacogdoches. If he had, I'd have answered yes, and for the first time in a long time, I'd have been telling the truth.

TIME

Many years ago the last building on the west end of Roatán, the largest of Honduras' Bay Islands, was a lantern-lit plywood shack called the New York Restaurant. From there you could stroll forty-five minutes along one of the world's most exquisite beaches without seeing another sole or structure. I'd snorkel between great walls of coral, and when schools of barracuda swam by me I wasn't scared because it was all too beautiful to be afraid. Afterward, I'd doze in the shade of one of the many palms arching over the white sand. One day, six untended horses moseyed by, stirring me from my sleep. Another day I was roused by the sound of splashing, and I sat up to see a trio of female Scandinavian backpackers frolicking nude in the clear water. It was like waking up inside a beer commercial.

The owners of the New York Restaurant would cook you a fresh snapper dinner for a dollar and rent you a room for a dollar more. Hammocks went for fifty cents, and the thriftier travellers would double up, some having sex in the hammocks, a pursuit that sounded more awkward than fun.

On one visit I was assigned Room 4. It had no ceiling, just an open space to the rafters. In the middle of the night I felt some plops on my bed. It rained most every night and I assumed the roof was leaking. But I came to realize the plops weren't raindrops. They were rats.

It was a new moon and very dark, and the rats scurrying atop the ceiling of the adjacent room apparently couldn't see. When they reached the end of the ceiling they plunged through the blackness and landed on me. They didn't feel like big rats, and I was in the grips of one of those tropical deliriums that make it hard to move, so I sealed myself beneath the lone sheet and let it rain rats through the night. In the morning they were gone.

I've never worn a watch except for this particular journey. It started as a joke. A newspaper I worked for merged with another paper. They needed to cut down on staff, so buyouts were offered to anyone who would quit, and I took one. If someone is going to pay me not to work, I'm not going to think about it too long. On my final day, the owners gave watches to those of us who had taken the buyout. They weren't nice watches—they were cheesy souvenirs. Their faces bore the company logo (a handbell) and motto ("the ring of truth"). I strapped mine on and played the parody of the company man who is presented a "gold" watch for time served.

I went to say goodbye to the editor who had hired me five years earlier. He was a *glasshole*. Glassholes were the senior editors who occupied the glass offices that surrounded the newsroom. He once let me get the word "tsunami" into seven consecutive stories, none of which had anything to do with tidal waves. Around the newsroom I became known as Tsunami Mike. This editor put a stop to my streak when I used the word to describe the upper anatomy of a shapely woman marching in a Christmas parade. On my last day, we shook hands and he told me what "a pleasure" it had been working with me. He'd grown ever more political and slippery through the years, but at least he owned it and delivered the line with a smirk. He wasn't that bad. For a glasshole.

"Hey," I said, tapping the face of my new watch, "know what time it is?"

"No, what time?" he said.

"Time to leave."

Now that I had no job or any schedule to keep, I'd somehow become dependent on that tacky timepiece. I wore it everywhere. But on the morning I woke up in Room 4 of the New York Restaurant, my watch was missing.

I ventured out to the patio and found Stass, the Garifuna caretaker. He had long dreadlocks and lazed in a hammock all day smoking blunts the size of cigars.

"Stass," I said, "I can't find my watch."

"Did you check your mind, *mon*?"

"My mind?"

"Yeah, *mon*, when we lose something, we usually only lose it in our minds."

Stass had a point. Maybe I'd forgotten where I'd left the watch.

I returned to my room.

I was fairly certain I'd placed the watch inside my shoe like I did every night. When I didn't find it there, I checked my duffel bag and daypack. The room had no dressers or shelves. The only furniture was the bed. I checked the folds of the sheet and overturned the mattress. There were no windows and the door had a latch. The case of the missing watch was like a locked room mystery.

After a bit more sleuthing, I reached the inescapable conclusion.

"Stass," I said, "the rats took my watch."

Stass took a deep hit from his blunt, exhaled and squinted one eye against the circling smoke.

"No, *mon*," he said, "rats don't care about time."

DISNEYLAND

The year my mother got hepatitis was when I first sensed there existed a greater world beyond the little one I occupied. I was seven and everything was suddenly exotic. We were renting in the Garden of the Gods, a working-class neighborhood on the outskirts of Sacramento, with street names like Adonis and Mercury and Thor. Lou, the husky woman two houses down, hailed from Louisiana. When you knocked on her door, she'd holler, "Come on in if your nose is clean!" Tommy Curieux, a fellow second-grader who lived on Morpheus Lane, was the first kid I knew with an *x* in his name. He said his ancestors were French and his family moved to California from some place called Maine, about a million miles away. I went to their home for dinner once. The dad was mysterious and wore glasses. The mom served us something called *cassoulet*. When I rode my bike home that night it felt like I was returning from a trip abroad.

    The doctors figured the toxins in the bottles of glass stain my mom worked with made her ill. She used to glue old drinking glasses together and stain them and sell them to crafts stores. But the garage was poorly ventilated, so her skin and eyes turned yellow. Next thing I knew, my dad, my little brother and I were lined up for gamma globulin injections.

The sound of the treatment—*gamma globulin*—petrified me long before I saw the business end of the syringe. The dose was apportioned according to your weight, so I kicked off my PF Flyers before standing on the doctor's office scale. The needle felt like it was a yard long.

The upside was that while my mom recovered we had a live-in maid. I thought only rich people had maids, so this new development was nothing short of astounding. The maid's name was Adele and she was African-American, although in those days African-Americans were still called Negroes. Adele was the first African-American I ever met, and now we were all living under the same roof.

Adele was alluring. She entered the kitchen each morning in her bathrobe, with bed-head hair and a drowsy smile. The first day she pulled out a skillet and made my brother and me French toast. We had never had French toast before and found it incredible. Every day after that one followed the same ritual: Adele would ask us what we wanted for breakfast, we'd scream, "French toast!" and Adele would say, "French toast, huh? Oh, okay." With our mom in bed and our dad at work, all rules were off. No more icky oatmeal. Before Adele, we never got dessert after dinner (except for a little Neapolitan ice cream on Liver Night), and now we were getting dessert every day for breakfast. Prepared by our very own maid!

It's funny how clearly I remember Adele, considering she was our maid for only four days. On the morning of the fifth day she woke my mom and asked for an advance. My mom wrote Adele a check for thirty-two dollars, her first week's salary. Adele gaped at the check as if she had just won the

Publishers Clearing House Sweepstakes. She waved it in the air and rushed to the phone on the wall in the kitchen. After an animated conversation with her boyfriend, Leon, she hung up and shrieked, "I'm going to Disneyland! I'm going to Disneyland!"

Leon pulled up to our house in an old dented Caddy. He had a thin, shiny scar on his cheek. Adele burst outside and ran across the lawn to Leon, waving her thirty-two dollar check over her head. Leon leaned against his car all cool-like, blowing smoke from his cigarette as Adele jumped up and down beside him, shrieking, "We're going to Disneyland! We're going to Disneyland!"

My mom, weak and yellow, emerged from the house in her bathrobe. "Adele?" she called in a soft voice, trying to get our maid's attention. "Adele, honey?"

But Adele couldn't hear her. "I'm going to Disneyland!" she continued to shriek. "I'm going to Disneyland!" She blew back by us into the house and came running back out with her suitcase. Leon took it from her and tossed it in the back seat.

"Adele," my mom called again from the porch. "Adele, honey, that check's no good."

But my mom's words wouldn't register with Adele. And in case anyone else in the neighborhood hadn't yet heard Adele's travel plans, she shrieked once more, "I'm going to Disneyland! I'm going to Disneyland!" Then she slid in next to Leon and they pulled away.

My brother said, "We getting a butler now?"

I knew all about postdated checks. Poor people wrote a lot of them back then. If you needed something you didn't have the money for, you wrote a future date on the check and said something like, "Could you wait until after next Friday to cash this, please?" In those days, at the end of each month, we'd be out of money, and my mom would return empty bottles for the deposits to buy a quart of milk. So in the end, I don't know which was the bigger fantasy: Adele thinking she was going to Disneyland, or me thinking we could keep a maid.

As Adele headed out on her big adventure, I knew she was bound for disappointment rather than Disneyland, but I envied her just the same.

FIRST DAY IN ANTIGUA, GUATEMALA

It was raining and the only locals in the park were the beggars and the afflicted, people with clubbed feet and abbreviated arms and faces hard to look at. A few *indígenas*, passed out on *aguardiente*, sprawled over the steps of the Palacio del Ayuntamiento. One rolled face down into a puddle in the cobblestone street. When I fished him out, he came up swinging.

I slipped into the nearest bar, where tourists watched a college basketball game on a TV tuned to a pirated satellite signal out of Houston. The owner's daughter, a precocious four-year-old, snatched the remote and changed the channel. The screen filled with a threesome scene from an adult film. The girl squealed until her dad, flushed with embarrassment, wrested the remote from her and clicked back to the game. A gringo entered the bar, wincing and shaking his hand. "I just decked an Indian," he said, and asked for a menu.

The streets turned to streams, and I sloshed a block and a half to a posada and checked into a two-dollar room. It was then I remembered the six grand stuffed in the bottoms of my wet shoes. I laid out the sixty soggy Benjamins on the bed and babysat them until they were dry enough to hide. I tucked the bills between the pages of a guidebook and in the cases of some music cassettes, as well as inside a roll of toilet paper, a box of Q-tips and an Old Spice deodorant applicator. The shower was electric and gave me a jolt when I grabbed the water handles, so I banged the knobs on and off with a plastic shampoo bottle.

My room faced an interior courtyard. The fellow in the next room had his window open. He was asleep. A boombox sat on his bed and a paperback—some African adventure novel—rested on his bare chest. He awoke and saw me staring at him and said, "Hey." He propped himself up against the pillow, and I noticed the bandage on his stomach. The guy ran a little import-export business in Texas. Two days earlier he'd had an emergency appendectomy. After he came to in the recovery room, he watched a Mayan choke to death on his own vomit and decided to take his chances at the posada.

The Texan saw me eyeing the iodine-stained bandage, and he struggled to the edge of his bed.

"Here, look," he said.

"Don't," I said, "you might get an infection."

"It's okay," he said, and pulled the bandage from his wound. There were only three crude stitches for an incision that stretched a good five inches across his gut. He looked like a scarecrow sewn together by a farmer short on twine. The middle suture was loose, and part of the incision had pulled apart. The Texan squeezed the fresh wound between his thumbs and index fingers. A deep narrow slit opened. I shuddered when I gaped into the space where his appendix used to be. The Texan smiled. Was there anything I could get him? He asked me to check in on him tomorrow, maybe bring him another African adventure novel.

Piles of lumber and rebar lay scattered in the courtyard. It was never clear whether the renovation was planned or already completed. A painting of a Hindu holy man with a jumbo Afro hung near the registration desk. It was a curious choice of art for a posada in the former capital of Spanish colonial Latin America. I asked the owner about it and she gave me a lengthy answer, which I couldn't understand because I didn't yet know her language.

I wandered back out to search for a Spanish teacher. It had stopped raining and Volcán de Agua was now in view. The volcano dwarfed the city, and the scene looked at once awesome and preposterous, like King Kong atop the Empire State Building. Stray dogs padded down the sidewalk. I scouted for footholds in the adjacent bougainvillea-draped wall, just in case. Earthquakes had destroyed this town several times through the centuries, and beautiful ruins now dotted every block. There were no billboards, neon signs or stoplights. The civil war still raged, but it was far away. I had no way of knowing it that day, but I would live here for much of the next three years.

WHICH WAY?

I saved enough money from Saudi Arabia to forget about work for a couple years. I decided to go back to college and get my degree. I set aside an amount to cover tuition and living expenses, and then invested the rest in South African gold mining stocks. When the price of gold doubled in two months, I had an even bigger cushion. It felt like I could coast forever. But before I knew it I was a college graduate with a dwindling bank account and no prospects.

I needed to find a career, a job at least. Instead I pissed away an entire summer in Davis, California, waiting for the lease to run out on my apartment. My old roommate left me his portable black-and-white TV. The cabinet was covered in denim. Most ridiculous thing I ever saw. It even had a pocket. I'd start each day watching the short-lived David Letterman morning show. Then I'd go play basketball and tennis for hours. At night I'd ride my bike into town and play lowball poker in the back of a ratty bar.

I had an afternoon ritual: I'd run out my front door and, after attaining full speed, leap as far as I could across the swimming pool in the middle of the apartment complex. My goal was to reach the other side. I kept getting closer and closer, and I may have made it had I bothered to first set down my beer.

I knew I liked to travel, so I applied with several airlines to become a flight attendant. There were two problems with this plan. For starters, I was four inches taller than the maximum allowable height. I fudged on my applications, but I knew I'd be found out when I turned up at the interviews. The other thing was that I had recently developed a fear of flying.

Flying was but one in a long list of fears. I worried a lot about serial killers and imagined them climbing through my bedroom window. I'd leave my front door unlocked at night so I wouldn't have to fumble with the handle when fleeing. Some mornings I'd awake in a panic, convinced I'd forgotten how to breathe. I was afraid I might swallow my tongue. A heart attack always seemed imminent. It was also around this time that I was seized by a fear of spontaneous human combustion.

One day a letter arrived. "Dear Graduating Senior," it began. I called the phone number. The folks on the other end were glad to hear from me and set up an interview for that afternoon. I guess it was boredom more than anything that led me to take the entrance exam for the United States Navy. Specifically, the exam was for college grads seeking a spot in the Navy's Officer Candidate School, or OCS. The recruiter, Bob, graded my test while he talked on the phone. He gave me a thumbs-up. When he got off the phone he told me I'd scored high enough to qualify for any program.

"Which way do you want to go?" he said.

All through junior high and high school, I worried about getting drafted. The Vietnam War dragged on and on. An antiwar poster captured my attitude about the military: "Join the Army! Travel to exotic, distant lands. Meet exciting, unusual people. And kill them." Yet there I was, in an armed forces recruiting office, talking about volunteering.

"I'll have to think about it," I told Bob.

He handed me a stack of brochures. "Don't think about it too long."

There was little chance of that. Bob called me every day. I always told him I was still "weighing my options." I never told him the truth—that I was closing in on my goal of hitting the other side of the pool. I stopped answering my phone.

That fall I headed out to seek work in resort management. My first stop was Sun Valley, Idaho, home of a world-class ski area. They offered me a job running one of the mountainside restaurants—generous, considering I had no restaurant experience at the time. I knew I wouldn't get a better offer, but I kept looking anyway.

Late one night, while waiting for a change of buses in Salt Lake City, I went for a walk. I was lonely and disoriented. A car pulled alongside me. I walked faster. The driver rolled down his window.

"Need a ride?" he said.

I figured the guy wanted to have sex with me or kill me, maybe both. I shook my head and kept walking. I peeked over my shoulder, but the car had vanished. I stopped for a hamburger. I returned to the Greyhound station and boarded my next bus. A relief driver sat behind the driver's seat. It was the guy who offered me a ride. It sure looked like him anyway.

I took a seat down the aisle and hoped the bus would fill up with other passengers. But the bus left with only a few riders. I stared at the back of the head of the relief driver. A half hour east of Salt Lake City, the bus exited the interstate. It was pitch dark and I couldn't see a thing. The bus sped down an unlit road. None of the other passengers appeared concerned. They had to be in on it. I reached in my knapsack for a weapon and found the Phillips screwdriver I carried back then. My eyes never left the relief driver. I didn't dare fall asleep, not even after the bus returned to the freeway. I sat there clutching that screwdriver until dawn.

Over the next few weeks, I traveled a big circle through the Rockies, riding buses and sleeping in cheap motels. When the money ran out I headed for my hometown, Tahoe City, California.

A building contractor hired me on. It was grunt work. They didn't even trust me with a hammer. One night after work I pulled out the Navy brochures. I studied the pictures of sleek ships cutting through blue water, and smiling men in crisp white uniforms walking arm in arm with gorgeous women in foreign ports of call. My hands itched from the fiberglass insulation I'd handled earlier at the construction site.

I called Bob the recruiter the next day and told him I knew which way I wanted to go.

"Outstanding!" he said.

It was past the deadline for the final OCS class of the year, but Bob said he'd "red-flag" my application.

Meantime, I reported to Oakland for my physical exam. I joined a long line of officer candidates and new enlistees. A bored medic drew my blood with hardly a glance. A couple minutes later, after the vein in my arm had ballooned to the size of a golf ball, I cut back in line to show the medic.

"I told you to apply pressure!" he snapped.

"Is that it?" I said.

"What do you want, a Purple Heart?"

After about thirty of us had filled paper cups with urine samples, we stood in a lab room awaiting further instructions. Nobody came for our cups for the longest time. Some men set down their cups, wandered off and returned.

"Hey," someone said, "is this your piss or mine?"

Bob got word of my acceptance into OCS two days before my class was to start. He swore me into the Navy in the parking lot outside his recruiting office. He then had me raise my right hand and re-create the oath while he snapped a Polaroid. Bob was beaming and extremely relieved. I was his only recruit that autumn.

I flew to Providence, Rhode Island. The Navy's Officer Candidate School for Surface Warfare was in Newport, about thirty-five miles south. My instructions were to take a Navy shuttle from the airport. If I arrived after the shuttle stopped running, I could take a public bus, and the Navy would reimburse me. Under no circumstances was I to hire a taxi.

My plane landed after ten at night. The Navy shuttle had stopped service. So had the local buses. I called OCS. The man who answered spoke in a rapid monotone, rattling off a jargon-filled preamble he no doubt repeated hundreds of times a day. He ended with, "This is not a secure line. May I help you?"

I explained the situation and asked if I could take a cab. He said to call back in a half hour.

The airport bar was packed three deep with alumni from Brown University, arriving in Providence for homecoming weekend. I ordered a draft beer. Several people asked me which year I graduated. When I told them I didn't attend Brown, they turned away. Everybody looked successful and confident, happy and beautiful. I drained a second beer and called OCS.

The same operator answered and repeated the same hurried greeting. I reminded him of my situation.

"Officer Candidate McIntyre, I'm afraid we're still trying to locate the officer who can authorize use of a taxi," he said. "Is there a number where you can be contacted?"

I gave him the number of the payphone outside the bar. He told me to "sit tight"—they'd get back in touch shortly. I waited by the phone another fifteen minutes. When nobody called, I returned to the bar and got drunk.

I needed to use the restroom. I asked a guy next to me to answer the phone if it rang. OCS still hadn't called when I got back to my barstool. I called and asked, why the holdup? The same young man told me they were still trying to "secure authorization" for a taxi. I hung up and ordered another beer. I thought of bailing on the Navy, maybe partying in Providence all weekend then heading back to California. That's when I remembered: I was already *in* the Navy. If I left now I'd be AWOL.

The last flight of the evening landed, and the bar emptied. I drank until the bartender gave last call. I chugged a final beer and sat down on the floor by the phone booth. All the airline counters were closed, and a janitor guided a polisher across the floor.

It was after midnight when the phone rang. The same young man said excitedly, "We've secured authorization." He sounded like America had just won a war. I was to hook up outside with two other late arrivals and share a cab to OCS.

The other two officer candidates chatted rapidly on the drive to Newport. One of them was named John. He was twenty-nine, the cut-off age for OCS. He had a wife and two kids in Ohio. His knee kept bouncing against mine, and I could almost smell the fear on him.

The cab pulled into OCS. I got out and glanced around. The place resembled a college campus. This might not be so bad, I thought.

A man in uniform appeared from nowhere.

"Cage those eyes, mister!" he barked.

The command stunned me. This wasn't how OCS was portrayed in the brochures Bob gave me.

The officer marched us inside for processing. The building was silent. Several hundred other officer candidates had already completed processing and turned in for the night. I was tired and drunk and only wanted to find a bed. I'd figure out the rest in the morning.

We were each handed a blank index card. An officer told us to fill them out exactly like the example on a nearby chalkboard. I carefully wrote down my answers according to the sample and handed in my index card.

An officer read my card and said, "Outstanding."

The other two candidates had to re-do their cards over and over. They wrote in cursive rather than block letters, or they'd put their Social Security number or date of birth on the wrong line. An officer announced that none of us could go to bed until we had all filled out our cards properly. This made the other two candidates even more nervous, and they each loused up a few more cards before getting it right.

The other two candidates each carried two suitcases. I had only a daypack.

"Is that all your luggage?" an officer asked me.

"Yes, sir," I said.

"Outstanding, O.C. McIntyre."

I saw no point in telling him the airline had lost my luggage.

We were each issued two sheets, a blanket and a pillow. Yet another officer marched us down a long hallway. He kept us an inch from the wall. Whenever I peeked sideways, he yelled, "Cage those eyes!" He dropped the third guy in our group at a room, and then marched John and me to another room. We were to be roommates.

The officer ordered us to make our beds—"racks," he called them. He told us to sleep *on top* of the blanket. I looked at him inquisitively. There wouldn't be time in the morning to make our beds, he said. As soon as he left I crawled under the covers. I pulled my alarm clock out of my daypack and set the time. It was two a.m. A rack never felt so good.

I awoke with the worst hangover of my life. My eyes burned. It felt like I had just closed them, which I pretty much had. My alarm clock read five a.m. It was hard to sleep through the rude sound of a metal garbage can tumbling down the hallway. And the booming voice that accompanied it: "Officer Candidates! You have two OCS minutes to get on the line!"

I soon learned an "OCS minute" was a duration considerably less than sixty seconds. And "the line" was the edge of the first row of linoleum tiles outside our doors. John and I fumbled for our clothes and rushed into the hallway. Officer candidates stood at attention outside their rooms. I saw some of my classmates were women, including the two candidates across the hall. One of them was an extremely attractive brunette.

Officially, I was enlisted in the U.S. Navy, but I had an out. An officer candidate could quit any time up until the day he received his commission. My plan that morning was to drop out of OCS, find a motel and go back to sleep. But standing there on the line, my eyes caged on the brunette across the hall, I had second thoughts. I couldn't quit in front of her.

Officers paced the hallway, pausing to inspect each of our rooms. An officer emerged from my room and ordered John and me to follow him back in.

"Whose rack is that?" he said, pointing to the mound of twisted sheets and blankets.

"Mine, sir," I said.

While my fellow officer candidates waited on the line, I was instructed on the proper procedure for making up a rack. I was again advised to sleep on top of the blanket.

An officer gave us five OCS minutes to "shit, shower and shave." The few women on our wing were led to separate facilities. The rest of us raced down the hall in slippers and bathrobes to the men's head. There were two toilets, six showers and four sinks for sixty officer candidates. When we returned to the line I had shampoo in my hair and shaving cream on my face.

We had ten OCS minutes to eat breakfast. I was so hungry I forgot about quitting the Navy and chowed down. Next stop was the barber, who sheared me like a sheep. We were handed a stack of books on subjects like engineering and navigation. We were measured and issued uniforms. They were covered with loose threads, known in Navy parlance as Irish Pennants, or IPs. We spent the next couple hours plucking IPs from our new clothes.

Then we marched.

Our wing leader, a huge man who threw the garbage can down the hallway, marched us back and forth over expansive lawns. It was November, and an icy wind blew in off the Atlantic Ocean. There were a dozen other groups marching across the lawns. We were all learning to walk again.

We marched and marched. We plucked more IPs. We scarfed meals in ten OCS minutes, and shit, showered and shaved in five. There was never any time to quit. I guess that was the idea.

On my second night we were issued officer's hats. We had five minutes to assemble the hats in our rooms then get back on the line. Assemble? I thought you just wore a hat. But there was this yellow band I couldn't figure out. John got his hat together, no problem. He asked if I wanted help. The guy I suspected would hightail it back to Ohio was turning into a

Navy man. I told him, no thanks, he'd better get back out on the line.

Our wing leader bellowed out my name. I was the only one missing from the line. He entered my room. I stood there grappling with my hat, pretending to put it together, but I was clueless. The wing leader snatched the hat from me, swiftly assembled it and passed it back. I felt pathetic.

The following morning—my third at OCS—the entire wing stood at attention on the line. I realized there was never going to be a free moment when I could discreetly pull someone aside and say, thanks, but I'm ready to go home now.

I surprised myself when I called out, loud and clear, "Officer Candidate McIntyre requests permission to speak."

The brunette across the hall shot me a startled look. At dinner the night before, she told me I'd helped her get through the first two days. Every time we went out on the line, she said, she stared at my Adam's apple. She said I had a nice one; it kept her going. But now my Adam's apple and I were about to let her down.

The wing leader strode over to me. He stood a head taller. He leaned down and put his face about an inch from mine. I could feel his breath.

"Speak!" he shouted.

"Officer Candidate McIntyre requests permission to disenroll," I said.

They didn't waste any time. I was off that wing in a hurry, cut out like a cancer.

They took me to the enlisted bachelors' quarters, where I found the many other officer candidates who were quitting.

My new roommate was a former deputy sheriff from Wichita, Kansas.

"My boss tells me I can have my old job back," he said. "I called home this morning. I told them I really missed them at work."

There was nobody barking orders, no one yelling at us to cage our eyes. There was no line to toe. We could come and go as we pleased. We could spend as long as we liked in the cafeteria. We could shit, shower and shave all day if we wanted to. We were now government waste, the human equivalent of the six-hundred-dollar toilet seat.

I killed time with several others who were in various stages of disenrollment. We'd hit the base bar at night for beer and games of pool. There was a buxom blond from North Carolina. She talked sweetly and called me her "bunny." Everybody was confused. No one knew what came next. After a few nights I stopped hanging out with them.

I needed ten signatures to get out of the Navy—from a petty officer up through the base admiral. Each signature came with questions, lectures and sometimes a severe scolding. There was a lot of good cop/bad cop to the process, and it was surprising who played each role. The base chaplain accused me of never finishing anything I started. He called me a quitter. He scrawled his signature on my disenrollment form and told me to get out of his sight, spittle flying from his mouth. Others tried logic. Sure, the Navy had rules, their arguments went, but so did every job.

The signatures had to be gathered in order. It was taking longer than expected. People weren't always in their offices.

The weekend came and I was still in the Navy. I decided to get away from the base for a couple days. Before I left I gave the shoes I bought from the Navy to a grateful enlisted man in the bachelors' quarters.

I hopped a bus for Boston. It was the weekend of the annual Harvard-Yale football game. I strolled around Cambridge, staring at the pre-game parties unfolding beyond the windows of the splendid homes.

Outside the stadium, alumni decked out in fur coats mingled under tents, munching hors d'oeuvres and sipping champagne.

On Monday morning I walked into a skyscraper owned by an investment corporation and rode the elevator to the top floor. I told the receptionist I was there for a job interview.

A few minutes later a woman in a business suit appeared.

"I want to be a stockbroker," I said.

I was wearing corduroy pants and an old tweed jacket two sizes too big. I had a ridiculous haircut and no résumé.

The woman frowned.

"There are no jobs here," she said.

When I got back to the base, there were several messages from Bob the recruiter. My dad had called, too, so I knew the Navy had told him. I didn't return any of the calls.

Every officer whose signature I needed tried to talk me out of quitting. The second-to-last officer I met with was a captain. He originally wanted to be a doctor, he said. He planned to go to medical school after his commitment was up, but he stayed in the Navy because he was having so much fun. He was the only one who got through to me. I felt the words, "Okay, I'll stay," forming in my mouth. Then I recalled I'd given away my shoes, and I changed my mind.

I collected my tenth signature and headed for the disbursement office. They gave me a choice between a plane ticket home and a mileage payment. The mileage rate back then was thirty cents per mile—or roughly one thousand dollars for my return to California. One-way, coast-to-coast airfares were only about one hundred dollars. I took the mileage payment and pocketed the difference.

Thanksgiving was two days away, but I was too ashamed to go home. I rode a bus to New York and checked into the YMCA on West 34th Street. On Thursday morning I watched the Macy's Thanksgiving Day Parade on the tiny black-and-white TV in my cell of a room. When I heard the commotion outside my window, I looked and saw Rocky and Bullwinkle floating down the street below.

That afternoon, I walked to a hybrid cafeteria-bar a few doors down from the YMCA. A football game played on the TV. I took my plate of turkey and mashed potatoes and gravy to the bar and ordered a beer. An old rummy sat a few stools over. He scooted down and joined me.

"So you don't have anybody to spend Thanksgiving with either," he said. It wasn't a question.

His name was Joe, and his nose looked like an enormous strawberry. I thought he might weep.

"The whole family is over in Jersey eating turkey," he said, staring into his cocktail. "But not Uncle Joe. Nope. Nobody wants to spend Thanksgiving with Uncle Joe."

On Friday, the day after Thanksgiving, I saw the new Robert De Niro film, *Raging Bull*. It was still daylight when I left the Midtown movie theater, but the world had changed. I walked down Seventh Avenue and thought I was going to kill myself. I wasn't suicidal. It felt like something that was beyond my control.

A crazy man jumped into my path. He got right up into my face and shouted something unintelligible. Then he hit me with an orange balaclava. I ran away, and the crazy man chased me. The sidewalk teemed with Christmas shoppers. I tried to disappear into the crowd, but the crazy man was locked in on me. He sliced through the stream of pedestrians. Every time he caught up to me he yelled and whacked my shoulders with that orange ski mask. I raced down the block. I paused at the next intersection. I didn't know which way to go.

CUSTOMS

"Customs tell a man who he is, where he belongs, what he must do. Better illogical customs than none; men cannot live together without them."
—Robert A. Heinlein

BHUTAN'S NATIONAL SPORT

Andrea and I had barely left the terminal at Paro Airport before pulling over to watch our first archery match. Archery ranges in Bhutan are 165 yards long, and since flat ground is scarce in this tiny mountain kingdom, they share space with roads, school playgrounds, even airport runways. People and animals simply go about their business as arrows fly overhead.

Archers, like most men in Bhutan, wear a *gho*, the traditional pleated robe, worn with a belt and knee-high socks (often argyle). Teams place half of their archers at each end of the range and shoot arrows back and forth at targets the size of dinner plates. When an archer hits the target, he and his teammates break into song and dance. The day after our arrival, the national championships were completed in the dark because celebratory singing and dancing stoppages had delayed the competition by a cumulative forty minutes.

It's okay to taunt and distract the other team. As the archer draws back his bow, his opponents lean in close and shout the local equivalent of "Miss it, Noonan!" Some smart aleck downrange will stand in front of the target, mocking his opponent's skills. Naturally, mishaps occur—the smart aleck loses sight of the incoming arrow, or teammates still celebrating an earlier bullseye aren't paying attention, and somebody catches one in the chest.

One morning the sports page carried a story about a young archer who was hit square in the forehead by an arrow and lived. Rather than yanking the arrow out on the spot, which may have caused the archer to bleed to death, his teammates delivered him to the local medical clinic. None of Bhutan's physicians are specialists, but all are experts in the extraction of arrows. (That said, a Member of Parliament had been recently airlifted to Kolkata, India, for an especially tricky extraction.) Bhutan's Department of Youth, Culture and Sports was waging an all-out campaign to educate archers on the perils of removing arrows from the body anywhere other than in a medical facility. Suggesting archers stand a pace or two farther from the target was out of the question.

When our return flight took off from Paro the following month, I glanced out the plane window to see the archers at the end of the runway raising their arms and waving goodbye to us with their bows. Or maybe they were still celebrating a bullseye.

A SAUDI SUPER BOWL

My most memorable Super Bowl Sunday was a Friday in April 1979. The one TV station in the Eastern Province of Saudi Arabia had evidently run out of religious programming and was broadcasting the game three months late. Pittsburgh and Dallas were playing at the Orange Bowl in Miami. And there we were at the Sand Bowl in Al Khobar—122 degrees and 99 percent humidity.

It was a Muslim holy day—a day off for my ten Western co-workers and me. We had our illegal ham, our illegal Scotch and my illegal bathtub beer—a nasty concoction as thick, dark and potent as OPEC crude. Praise Allah!

Nigel was there, too. Nigel was my pompous roommate—a British version of Charles Emerson Winchester III on *M*A*S*H*. The only tolerable thing about Nigel that day was he had invited to our villa a British Airways flight attendant named Penny who was laying over in Dhahran.

Nigel, dressed in a Union Jack T-shirt, launched into a surly attack on anything American. When his Yank-bashing degenerated into a denunciation of football, I could take no more. I issued a challenge: a goat race at halftime.

A muezzin in a nearby minaret was calling the faithful to prayer when Nigel and I mounted two goats owned by our

Bedouin landlord. (His two camels were asleep in the back of his Toyota pickup.) Penny stood fifty yards down the dirt road, waving Nigel's Union Jack T-shirt like a starter's flag at the Indy 500.

My goat didn't budge. Nigel's took off like a bat out of Saudi.

Pittsburgh went on to win, 35-31. Nigel went on to win, too. He was singing "Rule, Britannia!" as he melted into the shimmering heat waves.

WRESTLING MY CONSCIENCE

A huge crowd gathered outside the *plaza de toros* in San Cristóbal de las Casas, Mexico. It wasn't bullfighting season, so I asked one of the food vendors near the entrance what was going on. The woman looked up from an enormous kettle of boiling water filled with ears of corn. *"Lucha libre,"* she said. The bullring was hosting a wrestling match. Of the Hulk Hogan variety. I paid for my corn on the cob and headed for the ticket window.

A battered VW Beetle pulled to the curb, and four men hopped out. They were scrawny, but I knew they were wrestlers. Their masks gave them away. Ghastly disguises that made them look like medieval executioners. It was hard not to laugh as the puny pro wrestlers flounced toward the bullring. When I thought the scene couldn't grow any more absurd, two boys rushed up and asked for my autograph.

"Nitron! Nitron!" they yelled, jumping up and down. *"Autógrafo, por favor."*

"Cómo?" I said, thoroughly confused.

The bigger of the two boys handed me a flyer promoting the wrestling match. I saw the image of some gringo wrestler named Nitron. *"Ídolo de los niños,"* the flyer read. The boy pointed at the picture, then at me. A smile spread across his face. "Nitron! Nitron!" he shouted.

I studied the picture. It was small and grainy, but I could see Nitron had light hair and a fair complexion. It made sense. I was the only gringo around. Maybe in the eyes of a Mexican kid we all look alike. The two boys kept jumping up and down, screaming, "Nitron! Nitron!" I thought they might pee their pants, like I would've at their age had I met my boyhood idol Sandy Koufax. I considered telling them, yes, I was the great gringo wrestler Nitron. But I instead handed back the flyer and told them the truth. Their little shoulders slumped.

The smaller boy suddenly brightened. *"Conoces a Nitron?"* he asked me. This also figured. The only gringo at the wrestling match was bound to know Nitron. My answer again brought disappointment. The boys' heads hung low as they shuffled off. I didn't feel too good myself.

I bought a ticket and passed through the turnstile. *"Amigo,"* someone called. I turned and saw the two boys eyeing me through the fence. They looked at once sad and hopeful. I don't know why, but I assumed they had tickets. Here was my chance to be the hero the boys thought I was. If I couldn't be Nitron, if I couldn't know him, at least I could spring for the boys to see him.

I called them over. *"No tienen entradas?"* I said. They shook their heads. I reached into my pocket. I was about to pull out a wad of pesos when I looked up. The boys were now surrounded by thirty other young, ticketless Nitron fans, all of them staring expectantly at me through the fence. I froze. I didn't have enough money to treat them all. Nobody moved. I grew flustered and blurted out the first words that came to mind, *"Dónde están sus padres?"* I withdrew my empty hand from my pocket. The two boys studied me. I turned and entered the bullring, too embarrassed to face them another second.

I found a seat in the crowded nosebleed section. Vendors worked the bleachers, hawking hideous souvenir wrestling masks with demonic designs. Every kid begged his parents for one, and every parent seemed to give in.

A crude wrestling ring stood in the middle of the dirt bullring. It looked like it had been carted around for decades. The mat was ripped and duct-taped in places. It bore the faded corporate logo of Banco Serfin. I laughed at the thought of Bank of America sponsoring pro wrestling in the United States. Rows of folding wooden chairs surrounded the wrestling ring. They remained mostly empty, presumably because few could afford the 25,000 pesos it cost to sit in one. The battered VW Beetle I saw outside was now parked in the bullring. A conical speaker rested on its roof. The driver-cum-announcer sat behind the steering wheel and spoke into a microphone. What squawked out of the speaker was rendered incomprehensible by static and feedback.

My mind drifted to the boys outside the fence. A Mexican wrestling match is the last place I'd expect to engage in a moral debate with myself. Yet there I sat, pondering the dilemma: If I bought tickets for the two boys, I'd disappoint thirty other youngsters; but if I didn't buy tickets for anyone, nobody would be happy. I decided to follow my original impulse.

I returned to the front gate. I walked along the fence, back and forth, looking for the two boys. I felt sick when I realized they were gone. They probably thought I was some big jerk, teasing them when I reached into my pocket. Just another Ugly American.

But wait! Who was that over there, near the wrestlers' bus that had just pulled up? Jumping up and down in front of the tinted windows, trying to steal a peek at that wrestling god Nitron? Yes, it was them!

I waited for the wrestlers to leave the bus, knowing the two boys would follow them to the gate. I hoped I could get their attention before their thirty buddies showed up. The bigger of the boys spotted me through the fence. He beamed with recognition but instantly looked away, perhaps suspecting another gringo trick. He gripped a bar in the fence as he watched the masked wrestlers pass through the turnstile. I tapped his hand. When he looked up at me, I passed him a twenty thousand-peso note through the fence. His eyes grew big. He shoved the hand with the money into his friend's stomach and pushed him toward the ticket window.

I figured that was the last I'd see of the boys, but a couple minutes later they found me in a crowd of thousands. They squeezed in on either side of me in the bleachers. I worried they were sitting next to me out of obligation. I asked if they wanted to sit with their friends, but they assured me this was where they wanted to be. Introductions were made. José, the bigger boy, was twelve and Javier eleven, but both looked much younger. José wore a dirty white sweatshirt with the words "Love Savage." The boys couldn't contain themselves.

They squirmed and prattled on about the big event. This was their first wrestling match. I bought strawberry sodas for José and Javier and a beer for myself. Sitting in the bleachers with them reminded me of the time my father took me to my first baseball game.

There were seven bouts. The wrestling resembled the spectacle I'd seen from time to time on American TV—only much worse. There was the predictable "gouging" of the eyes while the ref's back was turned and the "slamming" of heads into the turnbuckles. I recognized two of the wrestlers who had exited the VW by the curb. They were paired as a tag team. Their opponents pinned them within seconds. But the pin doesn't mark the end of a professional wrestling match—it's the beginning. The winners threw the losers out of the ring. They rubbed their faces in the dirt and "smashed" chairs on their backs. And, the ultimate indignity, they ripped the masks from their faces.

The next wrestlers wore capes like cartoon superheroes. Then came the tag team of Solomon and Aaron Grundy, a pair of 350-pound bearded hillbillies who wrestled in overalls. I remembered these guys from TV. I guess Mexico is where washed-up wrestlers go, the way aging American baseball players end up in Japan in the twilight of their careers. I had never heard of Nitron, but I figured he must have washed out of the American circuit as well. I don't know how a wrestler washes out. Wrestling fans are fickle. Who knows, maybe Hulk Hogan will end up doing body slams in an obscure Mexican bullring.

The crowd was enthralled, especially José and Javier, who acted like they were at the New Orleans Superdome watching The Hulkster himself. There was a tag team match with four women. I had never seen this. It wasn't all that physical, mainly a lot of posturing to the frenzied fans. All the while the announcer kept up his inaudible commentary from inside the VW. I asked José when Nitron was going to wrestle. *"El último,"* he said. I guess they were saving the best for last.

The bouts dragged on for hours. The sun dipped below the rim of the bullring. It was growing dark. I noticed the arena had no lights. How would Nitron see? I soon got my answer. Two men dragged out a single lamp and stood it in the dirt next to the ring. It was like illuminating a theater stage with a flashlight. The announcer tried to help. He started the VW and turned on the headlamps. The beams shined *beneath* the raised wrestling platform.

Moments later, the crowd was on its feet, pressing forward, leaning over to catch a glimpse of the wrestlers who now emerged from a tunnel below the bleachers. Then there he was. Prancing behind the wall that protects matadors from the bulls. Passing just out of reach of his fans. Nitron. I didn't look anything like him. He had to be six-eight and weigh three hundred pounds. He had a blond mustache and a shag haircut. Instead of a mask he wore a sneer.

It was nearly pitch dark when Nitron stepped into the ring. José, Javier and I squinted, but it was impossible to make him out. If the boys were dejected, they didn't show it. They appeared ecstatic merely to be in the vicinity of their idol. Nitron's opponent was another gringo named Black Magic.

The only signs that a wrestling match was underway were some snorts and grunts and the dull thuds of bodies slamming against an invisible mat. Almost as soon as it started, a bell rang and it was over. I don't know who won. Probably the headliner, Nitron. That's how it usually works.

As Nitron made his way back through the blackness toward the tunnel, hundreds of kids crushed into the bottom row of the bleachers. They reached over the wall. They hoped to touch their idol, perhaps shake his hand, maybe get his autograph. Nitron strutted past, pausing only long enough to hawk a loogie at his adoring young fans. The crowd surged and I lost my balance. When I recovered, I asked José and Javier what they thought of their first wrestling match. But they were gone. Two little ghosts off into the night, chasing a giant gringo shadow, screaming, "Nitron! Nitron!"

DAY OF THE DEAD

On *Día de los Muertos* in Santiago Sacatepéquez, Guatemala, locals gathered in the cemetery to honor and commune with the dead. The cemetery overlooked rolling green hills quilted with crops. Families climbed atop vibrantly colored tombs and adorned them with wreaths, flower petals and pine needles—then sat down for a picnic with the departed. Many feasted on *fiambre*, a traditional cold stew of meat, seafood and vegetables.

Ice cream and beverage vendors rang bells as they wheeled their carts between the graves. I bought a bottle of Gallo beer and scaled an untended tomb.

The sky was filled with hundreds of homemade kites. In a few towns of Guatemala's central highlands, the *Feria del Barrilete Gigante*—giant kite festival—is a traditional part of Day of the Dead celebrations. Many participants fly their kites from the tombs of their ancestors to honor their memories.

The kites were fashioned from scraps of multi-colored tissue paper glued together in intricate patterns. One bore the image of Rigoberta Menchú, the indigenous Guatemalan woman who won the Nobel Peace Prize. Some kites were sixty feet in diameter, with lashed bamboo poles for frames. They were flown with rope instead of string, and their tails were made with the legs from tattered trousers.

The graveyard swelled with spectators. Children ran through the cemetery, jumping over graves and the lines of downed kites.

I glanced down and noticed a gravedigger digging a fresh grave. He grew distracted and his shovel strayed.

"Look, there's a skull!" someone said in Spanish.

Another exclaimed, "There's a femur!"

Someone else said the plot's occupant probably wouldn't care, and onlookers erupted in laughter.

Meanwhile, two dogs got frisky on the lip of the new grave.

The clouds gathered fast and burst. Everybody ran for cover. Soon the cemetery was empty. All that remained were scraps of wet tissue paper—and two dogs humping in the rain.

SUNDAYS IN BUDAPEST

We usually started with a bottle of sparkling wine and a tin of caviar, bought from the cramped market around the block from our flat in the Buda Hills. The wine came from Etyek, a village a half hour west of the capital, and the caviar was imported from Russia. My fiancée Anne and I were living paycheck to paycheck, and our paychecks were small. But Hungary was a real bargain in the first few years after the collapse of communism. The wine and caviar each cost about a dollar.

Late in the morning, we'd cross the Danube by tram to the Pest side of the city. We'd stop by an international newsstand, and if we timed it right, the UK papers would be in from the airport. We'd grab the *Times* and the *Independent*, as well as a saucy tabloid, like the *Sun*. Neither of us could read Hungarian. It was well before the era of online newspapers, and we were always starved for news from abroad.

We'd carry the papers to New York Bagels, at that time the only bagel shop in Budapest. Run by two Americans, it was housed in a high-ceilinged art nouveau building on Bajcsy-Zsilinszky út. *Diva*, by Annie Lennox, was the music of the moment, and if we lingered too long over our bagels and papers, we were liable to hear it three or four times. (More than twenty years later, I've yet to play that record again.)

After bagels, another of Budapest's yellow trams would deliver us to an outlying district, where we'd trudge through the sooty snow to a bowling alley. I don't recall how we learned of the bowling alley, but it was the only one in the city. It shared the ground floor of a small hotel. The chipped bowling balls and the shabby rental shoes appeared to have been on hand since the Hungarian Uprising of 1956. The shoelaces of the lone pair of size twelves had broken so often they were now a jumble of knots. The bowling alley had but two lanes, and they were always empty when we showed up. The right lane was flanked by the hotel's busy restaurant, with tables placed inches from the boards. The clank of dishes and the chatter of diners tested my focus during the running approach to the foul line. Had I been so inclined, I could've grabbed a bite of chicken paprikash on my way by.

Late in the afternoon we'd take in a movie at one of the city's many opulent theaters. The screenings were often lightly attended, as most citizens couldn't afford the one hundred *forints* (about seventy-five cents) for a ticket. Management assigned the seats. We'd invariably end up in a cavernous but near-empty cinema, packed together with the handful of other patrons. When Anne and I would move away from the pack to other seats, people would look at us like we were committing a subversive act.

Returning to the Buda side of the city, we'd switch trams or metro lines at Deák Ferenc tér, a popular square and transportation hub. Shortly after our arrival in Budapest the previous summer, a woman named Fatima arranged to meet us in that square. She said her family had an apartment for rent and she offered to show it to us. We could no longer afford a hotel, but our search for housing had led nowhere. When the appointed hour arrived, Fatima was late. Although she was a waitress we'd only met that morning, she acted sincere and helpful, and we didn't allow ourselves to believe she'd stand us up. We were so desperate that we held onto that belief as we scanned the faces in the crowd for the next two hours. Finally, I pointed over Anne's shoulder and exclaimed, "There's Fatima!" Anne whirled and, realizing Fatima wasn't there, managed a wan smile at my feeble attempt to make light of our predicament. After we had settled comfortably in Budapest, whenever we passed through Deák Ferenc tér, one of us would shout, "There's Fatima!" and we'd laugh. But a part of me always hoped to see her there.

We would often hook up with Sam and Lilly, a young couple from the U.S. we liked very much. They were in Eastern Europe seeking adventure, and, like Anne, only a couple years removed from college. They were plugged into Budapest's dynamic club scene. One time they tried to get us to stay out with them until dawn. Anne and I could only last until four a.m. As we climbed out of a smoky basement disco, Sam and Lilly danced and grinded atop an amplifier to a raunchy rendition of "Una Maz Cerveza."

One Sunday night Sam and Lilly came over to our place to chat and listen to music. I filled the fridge with these marvelous Czech beers the neighborhood markets used to stock. For good measure we also had a bottle of Pernod and some ice. Late in the evening, after working our way through all the beer and Pernod, the Cowboy Junkies' cassette *The Trinity Session* played on the boombox. When their haunting cover of the Velvet Underground's "Sweet Jane" came on, Sam and Lilly got up to go home.

"Let's all stand in the doorway and listen to the rest of this song," Sam said. "And when it ends, nobody say anything. We'll just leave."

Sam and Lilly grabbed their long winter coats and scarves and Russian fur caps. Anne and I walked them to the door. They stepped outside and turned around, Sam facing Anne and Lilly facing me. The strains of "Sweet Jane" spilled out into the snowy night. Toward the end of the song, Cowboy Junkies lead singer Margo Timmins sings a long loop of *La la la la, la la la,…* It lasts about forty-five seconds but feels much longer when you've agreed to stand in a doorway staring at your drunken friends and not speaking a word. Lilly looked up at Sam and grinned. Anne giggled. Sam stood ramrod straight and stone-faced, a hint of a smile playing at the corners of his mouth. I nodded with the music. At last "Sweet Jane" reached its final note and the cassette fell silent. Before the next song started, Sam and Lilly turned and walked off. It was the last time we'd see them.

The following Sunday night—after the sparkling wine and caviar, the papers and bagels and bowling, the movie and beer and Pernod—Anne and I sat on opposite ends of the living room. Another cassette tape had ended, and we rushed to fill the quiet space. Without discussing our dilemma, or even giving it a name, we had settled on a resolution.

Both of us cried.

"What are we going to do?" I said.

"We'll be okay," Anne said.

I shuddered and sobbed.

"You have good friends and I have good friends," Anne said. "We'll be okay."

I shook my head.

"We're not bad people, Mackie," Anne said through tears.

That's when I really lost it.

We had lived together in three countries over the previous eighteen months. To that point, it was the longest relationship of my life. We could no longer imagine a future together, but it was impossible to picture us apart. And yet... We gathered up the last of our black market German *marks* the next day, carried them to a travel agent, and booked separate flights back to the States. It was finally over.

Only it wasn't. Not yet. That's the funny thing about endings: sometimes you've got to try out a few before you find one that sticks.

THE CHICKEN IN THE CHURCH

At San Juan Chamula, in Chiapas, Mexico, I entered the brightly painted church on the plaza. The indigenous Tzotzil people who worship there are staunch Cafeteria Catholics. St. John the Baptist is the town's patron, and baptism is the only sacrament observed by the church. They don't even have a priest. When the need arises, the Tzotzils bring in a priest from another town, let him splash some holy water on the infant's head, then send the *padre* packing. The rest of the time, parishioners practice ancient Mayan customs with a few twists thrown in.

There were no pews in the church, and the floor was covered with pine needles. The air was thick with incense. Three Tzotzil women kneeled on the floor behind rows of burning candles. On the wall above, a costumed saint peered out from a glass case. Several mirrors dangled from the saint's neck. The women took swigs from bottles of Coca-Cola and belched in the direction of the saint. I couldn't see it, but apparently the saint relieved the women of their evil spirits by accepting them through the mirrors around his neck.

One of the women was sick. She pulled a live chicken from under her shawl. She stroked it and whispered something and snapped its neck. She placed the dead chicken on the pine needles. The three women chanted and belched some more. After a while, they packed the dead chicken in a plastic bag and left the church. Nobody would ever eat the chicken. The sick woman was now well, and the chicken now carried her disease.

A CROSS BETWEEN MARDI GRAS AND ARSON

I arrived in Luang Prabang a bit late—a good two or three years. The town had already gone Full Banana. Full Banana is when banana pancakes—the favored food of backpacker urchins worldwide—appear on one hundred percent of the local menus. Luang Prabang, a precious little peninsula at the confluence of the Mekong and Nam Khan rivers in Laos, is still magical. It's just no longer authentic. In the early morning, during the alms procession, more tourists than local Buddhists now place balls of sticky rice in the begging bowls of the passing monks. The monks and the townies, for whom the daily ritual is sacred, have become props in a silly photo op. Someday soon, tourists will actually be walking in the alms procession with the monks.

Fortunately, my visit coincided with the Ork Phansa festival, when Luang Prabangians took back their town with a vengeance, shoving tourists to the sidelines. The festival marks the end of Buddhist lent and features a raucous parade and every imaginable form of fire. It's basically a cross between Mardi Gras and arson.

In the days leading up to the festival, I got a preview of what was to come. The adolescent monks, who'd get to return to their home villages for the first time in three months, couldn't contain their excitement. They tussled, played grab ass and threw firecrackers at each other's heads. Now every monastery in town could be mistaken for juvie hall.

On the night of the big parade, each neighborhood wheeled its float to the staging area on the south of town. Their floats were boats, some as long as fifty feet, fashioned from bamboo and tissue paper. The bows and sterns bore the image of Naga, the sacred serpent. At the end of the parade route, the locals would launch their boats on the Mekong, and all of the town's bad luck would drift away.

I wondered whether any of the boats would reach the river, for they all appeared to be engulfed in flames. Each float held an improbable number of candles and diesel-fueled lanterns. Just when you thought a boat couldn't contain any more flames, some guy would drag out a stepladder and place another pillar candle beneath the tissue-paper dome.

Costumed residents accompanied their floats down the street toward the judges' platform. In between were marching bands, masked acrobats and fire-eating revelers. All the while people shot off firecrackers and fireworks, mostly at eye level. Half-naked toddlers stood on the curb holding aloft rapid-fire Roman candles. Every few minutes someone would toss a small stick of dynamite into the crowd, and the concussion would knock us back into the storefronts. There wasn't anything malicious in this—it's just not considered a successful Ork Phansa unless a few eardrums bleed.

This flame fest is one of the biggest events on the calendar, second only to the annual Luang Prabang Volunteer Firemen's

Ball. Predictably, one of the boats burned up before it could be launched, and you had to wonder what kind of luck that neighborhood was in for during the coming year. But the other seventeen flaming floats—along with countless candlelit, floating floral offerings—reached the river, and for the remainder of the night the Mekong burned like Lake Erie in the '70s.

Meantime, hundreds of fire lanterns soared overhead. They looked like colossal burning condoms and flew as high as jetliners, until they crashed into the surrounding villages and forest.

I bought a fire lantern and let it fly. Kids tried to shoot it out of the sky, their firecrackers glancing off rooftops, palm trees and power lines. You're supposed to make a wish when you release a fire lantern, so I wished for rain.

HALLOWEEN AT WORLD'S END

The ranger advised me to hire a guide for the six-mile trek through Horton Plains National Park, in the mountains of Sri Lanka. I'd already dropped thirty bucks on the park entry, and a guide seemed excessive. But there were wild boars and the odd leopard in the area, the ranger said, so at least wait and tag along with the next group of hikers. It was already seven in the morning. If I didn't reach the precipice known as World's End within the next couple hours, a wall of mist would block the view. No new hikers were arriving. I surveyed the wide trail that bisected the open grasslands. It didn't look dangerous. So I set out alone.

It was brisk and sunny, but the grasslands soon gave way to a thick forest, and I found myself enveloped in a creepy gloaming. The broad path narrowed to a rocky, muddy rut. Water coursed through the trough in some stretches. I hopped from boulder to boulder, trying to keep my shoes dry, as tree limbs scratched my face and roots snagged my feet. More than once I nearly toppled into the muck. I heard noises to my right in the dark woods and flashed on the scene from *The Thorn Birds* when Stuart is gored to death by a wild boar. My heart pounded in my throat. It was Halloween, and I was good and spooked.

I hurried down the trail. The next bend was about thirty yards away. When I rounded it, my view was limited to another bend in the near distance. I rushed through curve after curve, hoping each would lead to a clearing, but I was trapped inside a twisting tunnel. I thought of turning back, then cursed my fear. I came out of the next curve and froze in my tracks. Ahead lumbered a creature I couldn't identify, a hulking black apparition. Was it Sri Lanka's version of the Yeti? When I settled on the more logical conclusion—that I'd stumbled upon a sloth bear—I grew more afraid. The beast, sensing my sudden presence, stopped and turned to face me. What I saw came as a relief but still shocked me. It was an Arab woman, dressed head to toe in a black *abaya* and *niqab*, the traditional full-length cloak and face veil.

In Nuwara Eliya the previous night, I had dinner at the Grand Hotel, a heritage hotel near my guesthouse. The dining room was full of Saudi Arabian tourists. My waiter explained that the wealthy Arabs were the hotel's main source of revenue. They travel in droves to the Sri Lankan hill country to escape the heat of the Middle East. I stole a few glances at the Saudi women as they maneuvered slices of pizza and bottles of 7 Up under their veils. Dining out in that restrictive garb looked tricky enough. Trekking across steep, slippery terrain dressed like that looked treacherous. I hoped the woman was at least wearing sensible shoes.

She took a few more faltering steps down the soggy trail toward the next bend. Her foot slipped on a wet root and she fell hard on some rocks, splashing down in the muddy water. She winced and let out a little trill.

I resisted the urge to run to her aid. Many years ago I had lived and worked in Saudi Arabia. I knew that a culture that covered every square inch of its women didn't want men other than their husbands to look at them, let alone touch them. Especially Western men. Besides, no Saudi woman would be hiking through the forest alone. Sure enough, her husband returned from around the bend, followed by two boys. The family presented a stark contrast. Mom struggled on the ground in her cumbersome medieval costume while Dad and the boys freely bounded about in cargo shorts, hoodies and New York Yankees baseball hats.

I heard footsteps behind me. I turned and exchanged greetings with two Frenchmen carrying camera equipment. A Sri Lankan man, their guide, trailed them. I joined the guide, who appeared glad for the company. I gestured toward the Saudi woman sprawled in the mud. The guide rolled his eyes. "The water comes, they slip," he said. "Fall, fall, fall, always falling."

When we reached the Saudis in the middle of the trail, the guide scrambled by without looking at them. I followed, trying not to stare. But as I passed, I caught a glimpse of the woman and noticed she wore a veil with the narrowest of slits for her eyes. Once out of her sight, I held my hands over my eyes and replicated her field of vision by forming a tiny gap between my index and middle fingers. I immediately tripped and had to drop my hands to break my fall.

The guide and I discovered we shared a passion for golf. Before he was a guide, he caddied at the Nuwara Eliya Golf Club, founded in the nineteenth century by British tea barons.

He once played to a four handicap and had won the club championship several times. "Now I give the young boys a chance," he said, grinning.

We rounded a bend and encountered another scene like the one back up the trail: a Saudi mom splayed on the ground in her hazardous attire, tended to by a husband and kids who looked like they had just stepped from an Abercrombie & Fitch catalog.

After we passed the family, the guide shook his head and muttered, "Falling, always falling."

We continued along, and the guide explained how to play his golf course. "It is quite narrow, so you must be very straight, very straight," he said. "No slicing, no hooking."

"It might be too tough for me," I said. "I play a big draw."

I was about to expand on my golf swing when I spotted on the path ahead not one downed Saudi woman, but two.

"Falling, always falling," the guide said.

We stepped around the women as their more practically attired husbands arrived to assist them. The guide asked to see my golf swing, so I addressed an imaginary ball in the path and "hit" it. The guide saw my problem right away. I was coming at the ball from too far inside. If I wanted to stay out of the trees at his course, I'd need a more upright swing. "Like this," he said, demonstrating. He had a gorgeous swing.

We hiked another half hour, passing eight more Saudi women, only four of them standing. They sure were good sports. But I guess they had to be.

When we reached World's End, the guide rejoined his two French clients, who had already set up their camera equipment close to the edge of the precipice. He urged them to be careful. Two weeks earlier, he said, an Australian tourist plunged to his death there while snapping a photo.

I sat on the observation deck near a Brazilian couple and peered down the sheer cliff, fighting my fear of heights. Nearly three thousand feet below, the Walawe River looked like a length of silver thread. The river tumbled past tea estates, then meandered across the dry plains, where it entered a reservoir that sustained elephants and other wildlife at Udawalawe National Park, before emptying into the Indian Ocean. I ate one of the egg sandwiches my guesthouse had prepared and enjoyed the view.

A jolly group of hikers from Hong Kong emerged from the forest and traversed the windswept plateau to the cliff. "Is the world ending?" one of the men called out, drawing a big laugh.

By the time the Saudi families straggled up, the mist had rolled in and was obscuring most of the valley below. The women were never going to see much anyway—not with those blinders on. As they drew near, I saw their black cloaks were wet and smeared with red mud.

A Saudi family joined us on the observation deck. It was a small platform with no safety rails. A gust of wind caught the Saudi woman's abaya like a kite. She lost her balance and snatched the arm of her sensibly dressed husband. More Saudi families approached the precipice.

I didn't want to see any more falling this day. Not here. So I wrapped up my breakfast and started back down the trail.

MACHETES

I lived on the side of a volcano in Guatemala. In a tin-roofed shack with a pit outside to burn the toilet paper. This was before laptops and I didn't own a typewriter. I wrote at a rough pine table in longhand, in cheap legal pads of coarse paper the color of weak coffee.

When it wasn't going well, I littered the cement floor with wadded balls of false starts. At the end of the day I'd lean down and gather the balls of paper at my feet—but I had to be careful. That part of Central America was hot and humid, and when I'd leave the door open for the breeze, the occasional coral snake would slither in.

On some afternoons, when I was still lost in the story, I'd absentmindedly reach for the balls of paper, and seeing something move, I'd retract my hand faster than I thought possible.

The cure for a coral snake bite was the machete—clean through the bitten limb. All the workers from the neighboring *fincas* carried them—machetes—and they were quick to use them. There was no hospital, no clinic, no antivenin. Just the machete. Those workers thought they were doing you a favor.

That volcano, that shack, that cheap paper, the coral snakes, those machetes—it's still the best place I ever wrote.

THE ADUANA

The postman wouldn't deliver packages to my home in Antigua. They had to be collected from the customs house in the capital, Guatemala City, a two-hour return trip by chicken bus. The first time I showed up at the *aduana* with a package slip, a guard toting a machine gun led me to a warehouse. When a clerk finally appeared, she pointed to another clerk down the counter, who pointed to a third clerk, who ignored me. He read a newspaper and ate tacos, reaching into a drawer for a roll of toilet paper to wipe his mouth. After a while, he extended his hand without a word. I gave him my package slip. He passed it to a fourth clerk, who vanished behind a mountain of packages. He returned a few minutes later with my package. At last, I thought. But we were just getting started.

The taco-eating clerk opened the box with a knife and inspected the contents. I couldn't see inside. He reached for his calculator, jotted a number on a form, passed it to me and told me to pay the cashier. I was being charged sixty *quetzales*, about eleven dollars. Taxes, the clerk said. He showed me the customs declaration form that indicated the contents were valued at seventy-five dollars—I owed fifteen percent duty. I shook my head. The clerk said if I didn't want to pay the tax, he'd send the package back. Then he returned to his tacos.

I asked if I could look inside the package, but the clerk ignored me. I asked again. No answer. After my third request, he removed the lid and tilted the box toward me, just out of my reach. I craned my neck. It was a care package from the U.S., from Andrea. Photos, a few used books, some mixtapes and a back issue of *Time*. But what caught my eye were the shoes: a new pair of white Converse Chuck Taylor All-Stars, low tops.

I was on a bad luck streak with shoes. My only good pair had gone missing. My backup footwear was a decade-old pair of flip-flops, which had recently blown out. A cobbler tried to repair them, but the straps wouldn't hold. I was now down to a pair of disintegrating sneakers a gringo had left behind in Antigua. Guatemalan shoe vendors didn't carry size twelves. I could have had some custom made, but I was broke. I needed those new Chucks. I grumbled some more, but took the bill and headed for the cashier.

I complained to the cashier. The duty was exorbitant, nearly equal to the value of the shoes themselves. (This was before Chucks had evolved from cheap basketball shoes to the favored footwear of counterculture hipsters.) She told me to take it up with yet another clerk, who repeated the same fee formula. I told him the shoes weren't worth seventy-five dollars—it was a mistake.

"*Momentito*," he said.

He flagged down a passing man in a suit—the *jefe*. The three of us walked to the area of the counter where the clerk with the tacos guarded my package. A few more clerks edged closer. The jefe inspected the shoes, and I frantically made my case.

"Los zapatos son muy baratos en los Estados Unidos," I said. *"No son Air Jordans."*

Desperate, I raised one of my legs onto the counter. I pulled back the toe of the disintegrating sneaker and wiggled my foot. These were my only shoes, I told the jefe. Everybody laughed. I told the jefe I lived on fifteen quetzales a day. It was an exaggeration, though there were days when I lived on that little. "If I have to pay sixty quetzales," I said in Spanish, "that would mean—"

"Four fewer days," the jefe said.

"Yes!" I said. "Four fewer days in your beautiful country."

We both chuckled.

The jefe whispered something to yet another clerk, who typed out a new form. The jefe handed me my revised bill. The duty had been slashed to fifteen quetzales. I thanked everyone, even the clerk with the tacos, paid the bill and left before anyone changed his mind.

Out on the sidewalk, I kicked off my dilapidated sneakers and stepped into my new Chucks. It was the fifth time Chuck had entered my life in the last nineteen years: High school basketball, college, Saudi Arabia, Washington, D.C., and now Guatemala. Chuck and me. Me and Chuck. Together again. What a pair.

Two months later, I was back at the aduana. Friends from Oakland had mailed me a new pair of Teva sandals. I didn't see the guy with the tacos. The clerk who took my package slip must've thought I was a novice. He warmed me up to the idea of a bribe by asking whether U.S. Customs would charge him a duty on eight boxes of Guatemalan clothing. He pointed to eight nearby boxes.

"Probably," I said.

The clerk flashed a gold-toothed grin and said in Spanish, "Well, it's the same here."

He handed me a bill for seventy quetzales. But this time I had leverage—my Chucks. I set a foot on the counter and said I already had new shoes. Did the clerk care to buy the Tevas?

He asked how much. I said, seventy quetzales. He laughed and offered me ten. I said nope.

The clerk asked how much I'd be willing to pay in taxes. I held up both hands and said, ten quetzales. He countered with fifteen. I said ten. He said fifteen. I said okay.

I pushed a ten and a five across the counter. I said now I didn't have money for the bus back to Antigua. He pushed the five back to me and smiled.

HANGING IN PARIS

Paris was frigid that winter so we turned up the heat in our apartment. The heat gave me strange dreams, nightmares really. One night I was visited by a vision of what appeared to be a guillotine, set out on a cobblestone street in the Marais. But as I walked through the crowd toward the killing machine, I saw it was some newfangled gallows. In the morning I awoke to news of Iran's latest public execution.

Four young men on motorbikes had mugged a man in broad daylight on a street in Tehran. They attacked him with a knife but he wasn't seriously injured. The muggers escaped with the equivalent of twenty dollars. When security camera video of the crime spread to the Internet, the public reacted with outrage. The four men were arrested and hauled before Iran's top judge. The two ringleaders pleaded poverty, one claiming he needed money for an operation for his mother. The judge sentenced them both to death for "waging war against God."

At dawn one Sunday in January, police brought the two prisoners to a park in central Tehran. A crowd of three hundred watched as nooses were slipped over the muggers' heads. Iran doesn't use the long-drop method of hanging, which normally breaks the neck and leads to immediate unconsciousness. Instead, the condemned is slowly strangled to death while dangling from the end of a rope. After a court official read their crimes and the verdict, the muggers were hoisted fifteen feet in the air by two mobile cranes.

Over the years, I'd seen news stories and video footage of public hangings in Iran. The condemned were rapists, drug traffickers, robbers, homosexuals convicted of sodomy—but rarely murderers. Executioners typically positioned them atop buses and trucks, and they were left to kick and twist in the air after the vehicles pulled away. Lately the authorities had enlisted the crane. In some quarters that must've counted as progress.

What made the most recent hanging all the more chilling was a photo that accompanied the news article. Moments before the noose was secured around his neck, one of the muggers laid his head on the shoulder of an executioner and wept. The executioner, his face hidden by a black balaclava, placed his arm around the young man.

Andrea and I walked to the Marché des Enfants Rouges to find something to eat. Wandering the rows of food stalls, I was distracted by the thought of the hanging. When we returned to the apartment I searched the Internet for any new stories and photos.

In the ensuing days, this distraction turned into an obsession. Wherever I went, be it a movie in the Bastille or a stroll along the Seine, the execution was on my mind. I couldn't shake the image. I woke in the middle of the night and recalled reading that some spectators had filmed the double hanging with their smartphones. I sat up in bed and opened my iPad, searching YouTube for any videos. I was at once repulsed by the barbarity and somehow compelled to watch it. I tilted the screen at an angle. I didn't want the light to wake Andrea. I also didn't want her to catch me.

This went on for a week or so. Then one day, without realizing it, I'd forgotten about the hanging.

One afternoon I walked to the post office on Rue du Temple to mail a postcard. On my way back I decided to stop for a beer. Like much of Paris, this neighborhood is littered with cafés. I don't know why I picked the café I did—I just did. It was one I'd never been to.

I took a seat at the bar and ordered a Stella. A young couple snuggled in one of the leopard-skin booths. Above them, attached to the wall, was a full-sized mannequin dressed as a cowboy. He wore a cowboy hat, a denim shirt and a bandolier. A black-and-white photo of Barbra Streisand was pinned to one of his sleeves. And he had a noose around his neck.

CONFLICTS

"We are citizens of the world. The tragedy of our times is we do not know this."
—Woodrow Wilson

EXTREME SKIING

A busy campaign of genocide, mass executions, systematic rape and torture would seem to leave no time for skiing. But there the Bosnian Serbs were, making tracks in the mountains above the besieged capital of Sarajevo. Even war criminals and their minions needed a little R&R. More absurd, the Serb goons were inviting international tourists to join them on the slopes. Never mind that the civil war was in full swing and there were no flights into the former Yugoslavia.

"Our business is to offer skiing and accommodations," I was told by an official at Mount Jahorina, site of the women's alpine events when Sarajevo hosted the Winter Olympics a decade earlier. "How you get here is up to you."

My colleague Jim and I decided to take the Serbs up on their offer. We grabbed our skis and headed for Bosnia.

We were nearly turned back at Belgrade, Serbia. The local office for the Republic of Srpska, the name Bosnian Serbs gave their ethnically-cleansed territory, initially declined to issue us entry permits. It took two days to convince them we were only after some fresh Balkan powder.

The next trick was to find transportation. Avis refused our request to take one of their rental cars to the battlefront. We were referred to a man who agreed to drive us to Sarajevo for sixteen hundred dollars. Fuel was extra. Due to United Nations-imposed sanctions, gas fetched eight dollars per gallon on the black market, siphoned in dribs and drabs from the cars of Serbs who could no longer afford to drive. It took a few hours to secure enough gas for the 240-mile round trip, and we were off.

Once inside Bosnia, we drove past the charred and crumbled remains of several Muslim ghost towns, their former residents now either displaced or dead. Serb foot soldiers with Kalashnikov assault rifles patrolled the highway. We were stopped at a checkpoint and our driver rolled down his window. When a soldier pointed his AK-47 inside the car, I recalled what a friend had said when I told him I was going skiing in war-torn Bosnia: "That would be a *stupid* way to die, man." But the soldier saw our skis wedged between the car seats and laughed. The same scene played out at seven more military checkpoints, usually without the laughter. Finally, just outside Sarajevo, we turned left at a junction marked by an armored personnel carrier and climbed the road to the Jahorina Ski Center.

The sprawling complex of three hotels and six motels resembled an armed fortress more than a ski resort. Paramilitary forces, politicians and their families occupied most of the rooms. Bosnian Serb leader Radovan Karadžić and military commander Ratko Mladić, the Butcher of Bosnia, also bunked down there. It was from the ski center, as well as positions in the surrounding hillsides, that Serb rebels kept Sarajevo under siege for nearly four years. They assaulted the capital with artillery, rocket launchers and heavy machine guns.

Some of the soldiers who arrived at the main lodge's dining hall for dinner had spent the day killing civilians with sniper rifles.

Other signs that Jahorina wasn't St. Moritz: The Olympic flagpoles were flagless and rusted. The ski shop was out of sunscreen—and everything else. There was only enough fuel to heat the lodge a few hours a day, so residents wore heavy coats indoors. The casino was closed. The pool was empty. The toilet paper was rough and rationed. And of the mountain's thirteen ski lifts, only one was open.

Still, there was much to recommend the place. At forty-two dollars a day for room, meals and lift ticket, it was one of the last ski bargains anywhere. There was ample parking. And best of all, it was the only resort in the world where you could sleep in and still be assured of untracked powder at noon.

Resort manager Dragomir Blagojevic insisted a vacation there was as safe as a soak in a hot tub, but confirmed that Jim and I were the first visitors. He wore a camouflage jumpsuit. Like every other resort worker, Blagojevic was first and foremost a soldier. As he gave me a bone-crushing handshake I wondered how many Muslims he had killed. He was a Sarajevo native who'd worked on the technical staff during the Olympics. I told him we had something in common: I grew up near Squaw Valley, where the 1960 Winter Games were held.

"So then you can understand the misery that has come to my home," he said. "I hope nothing similar ever happens to your Squaw Valley."

He poured us shots of homemade plum brandy, then drank his from the bottle cap.

Blagojevic said that before the war, the bulk of the resort's international guests were Greeks and Italians. He figured many of those guests would soon be returning now that Jahorina was again open for skiing. I had to bite my cheeks to keep from laughing. I asked him why any tourist would want to come to Bosnia? He hesitated, then his secretary chimed in, "You can say you went skiing in a war zone."

On our one day to ski, we rose early and were greeted by a cloudless blue sky. A storm the day before had dropped a foot of fresh, dry powder. Word had it that the Serbs planned to open a second lift, which ran most of the way up the mountain where Americans Debbie Armstrong and Christin Cooper had finished first and second in the women's giant slalom in 1984. We carried our skis up the hill to the loading area. There was no one else in sight.

Eventually, Jim and I were joined on the slopes by a few dozen local skiers. Glances were exchanged among the Bosnian Serbs when they saw the first foreigners in a good while, but there was plenty of sunshine and powder for all. We made several runs in an open bowl of virgin snow. On our last run, we traversed through some trees and came out in the middle of a racecourse. Kids from the local ski team were running gates. Their coaches were soldier-fathers decked out in camouflage fatigues. Once the lifts closed, the men would climb back into their tanks and resume shelling Sarajevo. Like so much at Jahorina, the scene was surreal.

We loaded our skis into the car and headed down the mountain. The driver dialed in the news on the radio and translated for us. While we were skiing, a Serb shell had landed in Sarajevo, killing six Muslim children as they played in the snow. The sign at the ski resort exit read, SEE YOU AGAIN. It sounded like a threat.

WISHES

One morning in San Diego I sat at my bedroom desk in my underwear and scanned the Travel section of the classifieds. An ad jumped out at me: *"Pan Am voucher, good anywhere in the world, $200."* I dialed the number and learned why the price was so low. The guy who answered had been bumped from a Pan Am flight a year earlier. He'd forgotten that the voucher the airline gave him as compensation expired that day. Good thing for me few people can fly off at a moment's notice.

I grabbed my passport and hurried to the airport, where the guy met me with the voucher. I didn't know where I'd be flying, so I packed a duffel bag with both summer and winter clothes. My goal was to travel somewhere far that I had yet to see. The Pan Am agent told me India was out because I needed a visa. I wasn't up to date on my travel shots, so Kenya was a no-go. The flights to Tokyo and Auckland were full. So I settled on Israel, flying to Tel Aviv by way of New York and Paris.

I arrived in Israel during the run up to the First Gulf War. Citizens were tense. Saddam Hussein had threatened to attack Israel with chemical weapons. (Months later, after coalition forces invaded Iraq, Saddam fired forty-two Scud missiles into Israel, although none of them carried chemical payloads.)

Israelis waited in long lines for gas masks. When news reports declared the government was out of gas masks, I wondered if I was the only dude without one. I headed for the beach and did the elementary backstroke in the Mediterranean, trying not to dwell on the bombs that could soon splash down.

A couple days later I rode a bus to Jerusalem and inquired about a room at the American Colony Hotel. The receptionist said he had a vacant room for two hundred dollars. (As of this writing, rooms at this historic hotel, whose guests have included Lawrence of Arabia, Winston Churchill and Bob Dylan, run between $390 and $950 per night.)

"Do you have any less expensive rooms?" I asked.

"Yes, we have one hundred and seventy-five dollar rooms, one hundred and fifty dollar rooms, one hundred and twenty-five dollar rooms. Which kind of room would you like?"

"Do you have any forty-dollar rooms?"

Without hesitating, the fellow asked me to sign in and called for a bellman, who carried my duffel bag up to the most splendid forty-dollar room I've ever slept in.

I walked ten minutes to the Old City, entering through Damascus Gate. On the Via Dolorosa—said to be the path on which Jesus carried his cross to his crucifixion—I stopped to inspect a handprint on a stone wall. Christians claim this is where Jesus reached out to brace himself before falling under the weight of the cross. I don't know if this really happened, but it was powerful to see the deep palm and finger impressions from the centuries of believers who have rested their hands on this spot. I placed my hand into the embedded handprint. It didn't fit.

Inside the church where Pontius Pilate condemned Jesus to the cross, I tagged along with a small tour group to listen to their guide. The tourists appeared to be Europeans. There was a sudden commotion outside and I saw a mob of angry men rushing the entrance. We were in the Muslim Quarter and this was during the First Intifada. Security guards immediately closed the doors and fortified them with a plank. The Palestinians outside pounded on the doors and shouted, "Fucking Americans! Fucking Jews!" The plank bowed against the doors. I glanced around the small church and saw there was no escape. One of the tourists cried. "It's okay, it's okay," the tour guide reassured her. But I could tell from his nervous smile that it wasn't.

I never learned what dispersed the mob—whether Israeli forces intervened or the rioters left of their own volition. But it was quiet. Soon the security guards inside the church opened the doors and I was free to resume my stroll through one of the more contentious plots of ground in human history.

The Western Wall, or Wailing Wall, one of Judaism's most sacred sites, was surrounded by concertina wire and guarded by soldiers with Uzis. The faithful prayed and rocked before the ancient pile of stones. Someone told me the slips of paper stuffed in the crevices were prayer notes. I've never prayed but I've wished from time to time—birthday candles, dandelions, that sort of thing. There was something I wished for that day, so I wrote it on a scrap of paper. I reached high to wedge it between two stones so the great wish-granter in the sky might more easily spot it.

That afternoon I toiled over a letter in my hotel room. It cost a lot to send a fax to the U.S. then, so I wanted to keep it to one page. But there was so much I had to say—and to ask. When I thought I had it just right, I realized I'd written into the margins and the whole letter probably wouldn't transmit. The post office where the fax service was located closed at four o'clock and I feared I wouldn't make it. I urgently wrote a second version in smaller print and got to the post office just in time.

At Ben Gurion Airport an Israeli soldier pulled me from the Pan Am check-in line. She took my passport and asked me several questions: What was my occupation? Where had I stayed? Who drove me to the airport? Why had I waited until the day of my flight to buy my ticket to Israel? Why had I changed my reservation to leave a day early? When my answers didn't satisfy her she led me to a secure area and handed me off to her superiors, who searched my bag. They told me to snap photos of the ceiling and the floor with my camera, sip from my water bottle, taste my toothpaste. After two hours, the original soldier returned and accompanied me to the gate. She walked me all the way down the jetway to the plane, where I was the last to board. Only then did she return my passport.

"Why me?" I asked.

She smirked and said, "Everybody asks that."

When I landed at LAX my heart sank. The girl I loved wasn't there to meet me. That's the trouble with wishes—they don't always come true. It hurt for a while. But by the time my next trip rolled around, I'd learned there were better things to wish for.

SMILES

Southeast Asia struggled with its worst floods in fifty years. Flying into Cambodia, I saw entire villages submerged. Red tile roofs looked like gaping, bloody wounds beneath the surface of the water. Arriving in Phnom Penh felt ridiculous, like visiting New Orleans during Katrina. But what really threw me were the smiles. Why did everyone appear so happy?

The devastating flood was the latest in a long line of miseries to befall the Cambodian people. In my lifetime, they'd suffered through a secret bombing campaign, a barbarous revolution, forced labor camps, famine, torture, mass executions, and an endless cycle of crippling poverty.

This was my second trip to Cambodia, and I still couldn't wrap my head around the place. Nowhere else in the world had I encountered such huge measures of beauty and despair existing side by side. I found those smiles unsettling.

Yes, I realized Cambodia was decades beyond the Killing Fields. But I also knew that everyone alive had a link to the genocidal Khmer Rouge regime: they were the surviving victims or the relatives of the two million slaughtered or the slaughterers themselves. Few copped to that last category, but everyone knew who they were, and they were everywhere.

No one appeared in a hurry for justice. The brutal dictator Pol Pot got to die in his own bed in 1998, nearly twenty years after the end of the bloodbath he launched. It took another nine years before the other five members of his genocidal clique were rounded up to face a United Nations-backed war crimes tribunal. In four years, the tribunal had managed only one conviction. Two Swiss judges had resigned from the court due to government interference. Many of Cambodia's business and political leaders, including Prime Minister Hun Sen, had been mid-level members of the Khmer Rouge, and they feared what the tribunal might uncover.

Andrea and I checked into our hotel near the Royal Palace, and I flipped on the TV. A satellite channel aired a new documentary detailing the atrocities of the Khmer Rouge. A former Khmer Rouge executioner now living in the open reminisced about his killing technique. He slashed his victims' throats with a knife, he told the interviewer, pulling back the interviewer's head by his hair to demonstrate. On some days there were so many victims his hand cramped, the executioner said, so he switched the knife to his left hand and stabbed his victims in the neck. He told the interviewer he now felt "embarrassed"—and he smiled.

We took a taxi to the Tuol Sleng Genocide Museum, a former torture center known as Security Prison 21 (S-21). There we read the posted rules some fifteen thousand inmates were expected to follow on their way to forced confessions and extermination. Rule #6: "While getting lashes or electrification you must not cry at all."

The inmates, with identification numbers attached, were displayed on bulletin boards. One boy ... and his captors had fastened his ID badge to his bare chest with a safety pin. In the adjacent rooms victims were shackled, waterboarded, whipped, hanged, shocked and often raped. Some inmates were skinned alive. Others had organs removed without anesthesia. In some rooms you could still see bloodstains on the floor. Other than that the place looked like the high school it once was.

Outside in the courtyard we were introduced to Bou Meng, one of only fourteen prisoners who survived S-21. He was an artist the Khmer Rouge found useful because he could render vivid paintings of Pol Pot.

"If the portrait is not lifelike, you will be dead," his captors told him.

"Yes, brothers," Bou Meng had replied, "if it is not lifelike please beat me to death."

Meantime, Bou Meng's wife was killed at an extermination camp and their two children starved to death.

He stood behind a booth in the shade, selling copies of his biography, written by a local journalist. I bought a copy. Bou Meng signed the book and handed it to me with a smile.

Andrea and I rode a tuk-tuk out to Choeung Ek, the most notorious of Cambodia's three hundred former killing fields. We wore headphones and listened to an audio tour as we wandered past mass graves. To save ammunition, the Khmer Rouge had bludgeoned its victims with shovels, hoes and ax handles. Some soldiers cut out and ate their victims' livers and gallbladders, believing the organs would cool them on the muggy killing nights.

We stopped before a large tree where soldiers killed the children of Khmer Rouge enemies by bashing their heads against the trunk. The Khmer Rouge didn't want the children to grow up and take revenge for their parents' murders. A slogan of the revolution held, "When you dig up the grass, you must remove even the roots." Any sign of sympathy was suspect, so soldiers laughed as they killed. Some tossed live babies in the air and let them land on their bayonets.

I was numb by the time we reached the memorial stupa, a six-story glass structure filled with eight thousand human skulls. It was too abstract. Only when I stared at one broken skull, imagined the story behind it and multiplied that by eight thousand, did the enormity of the horror come into focus.

On the path leading from the stupa I spotted strips of faded material and white fragments poking from the ground. The recent floods had caused some of the victims' clothing, teeth and bones to boil to the surface.

Returning to Phnom Penh, our tuk-tuk was passed by a school van. Uniformed girls leaned out the windows, shouted hello at us and laughed. Good, I thought, this was their country now, or it soon would be. Maybe they'd put it to better use.

Days later, when we drove south on National Highway 3, we marveled at the Cambodians' creative and efficient use of scooters. One scooter listed under the weight of a family of five, the dad driving while the mom breastfed the youngest child. Two construction workers tore down the highway on a scooter with sheets of drywall and panes of glass resting on the seat between them. Another scooter driver balanced a pig on his shoulder with his right hand while steering with his left.

We stopped marveling when we saw the accident. There was no need to rubberneck, it was all instantly in front of us: the battered scooter, the bloody woman sitting in the road, the young boy with the cracked head dying in her lap.

Road fatalities are a good measure of a nation's level of development. Cambodia suffers from the highest rate in Southeast Asia. The potholed two-lane road we traveled had to accommodate trucks, buses, cars, scooters, tuk-tuks, bikes, ox-drawn carts and pedestrians. Safety costs so much. I realized why most of the Khmer Rouge were never punished. Justice, even revenge, is a luxury to people engaged in a race to survive.

We stopped in Kampot, a sleepy town of peeling French colonial villas, with sagging shutters, ceiling fans and geckos running the ocher walls. The cheery waif who checked us into the Rikitikitavi guesthouse told us her name was Ram Sual.

"But it's so hard to remember, so you can call me Rambo," she said. "Or you can call me Little Girl or Chickie or Puppet. What is your name?"

"Mike," I said.

"Make?"

"No, Mike."

"Oh, Make, like Make in China."

She drew her hands to her mouth and tittered.

"His name is Make," she said to another female employee, "like Make in China."

The two young women laughed, and for the rest of our stay I was Make in China.

Geckos, overhead fans and a kook named Rambo won't set the world right, but they can pull you out of a funk. For a while.

Andrea and I ate lunch in the terrace restaurant overlooking the river. I spotted a flyer on the wall for an upcoming concert by Dengue Fever, the Los Angeles-based Cambodian pop music band. We had seen them perform a few months earlier at the Casbah, in San Diego. I pulled out my iPad and played some of their music.

Suphat ("Pat"), the Rikitikitavi manager, recognized the music and joined us at our booth, sliding in next to me. He showed us a picture of his boyfriend, a middle-aged Englishman who had visited Kampot several years earlier. The boyfriend had returned to Cambodia often, putting Pat through the local business school and helping Pat's parents with living expenses.

When Dengue Fever's "Tiger Phone Card" came on, I sang along in English. Pat joined in, singing in the original Khmer. Now a duet, I took the female vocal and Pat sang the male vocal. When I came to the high part, Pat grabbed my upper thigh, prompting me to sing even higher.

Pat's father came from a family of twelve children. The Khmer Rouge killed all of his siblings and his parents. When soldiers rounded up his relatives, Pat's father knew they'd be forced to betray him. So he changed his name, disappeared into a work camp, and survived. Pat owed him his life. No matter how much he loved the Englishman, he could never leave Cambodia and his father.

On another day we hired a tuk-tuk driver named Rony to drive us through the countryside. In Kep, we feasted on crabs in one of the crab shacks jutting over the Gulf of Thailand. Afterwards we drove through a couple of the area's many pepper plantations.

Rony said most of his family survived the genocide. His wife was another story. She was a member of Cambodia's Muslim minority and all twenty-two of her relatives were killed.

We passed an oncoming scooter. Rony tooted his horn and waved at the driver, a blissful-looking woman who returned his wave and smiled. "My wife," Rony said.

Cambodia was heartbreaking. The place was so sad, yet so beautiful. I wasn't sure I could ever understand it. We decided to secure visas for Vietnam as soon as possible and leave.

On the morning of our departure Andrea woke up sick. I walked out to the street to meet the taxi Pat had arranged to take us to the border. I inhaled deeply, trying to stifle a sudden spasm of nausea. It didn't work and I rushed back inside to retch for the first time in ages.

We should have stayed but we knew we had to go. When we loaded our backpacks into the taxi, Pat drove up on his scooter to see us off.

"Good morning" I said. "How are you?"

"Not so good," he said, wincing. "My stomach is sick."

We climbed in the taxi and the driver pulled away. I looked back out the window and there was Pat. He held his stomach with one hand and waved with the other. And he smiled.

LIVE AND LET LIVE

In Tangier we sipped mint tea in a parlor of the La Tangerina guesthouse, an exquisitely restored *riad* in the kasbah that was once home to a Moroccan sultan. Andrea sat on the red sofa along with Steve and Gabriela, a San Francisco couple we met on the flight from Paris. I kneeled on the tile floor and stoked the fire with a pair of ornate bellows. Radio Swiss Jazz, an Internet station, played on the retro-style table radio. We had enjoyed a meal of harira, couscous and lamb tagine, and we were full and content.

The bliss was broken when a pair of loud Brits stumbled into the lobby, returning from dinner in the new city. One of them, Bill, a man of about sixty-five, was drunk. We had met earlier in the dining room, when he made a fuss about losing his room key. He was from Lockerbie, Scotland, and he had a big gut and a red, bulbous nose. He and his friend joined us in the parlor.

"How was the Italian restaurant," I said, trying to be polite.

"A bit of a con," Bill slurred. He grabbed the top of a wing chair to keep his balance.

"How so?"

"Just a bit of a con."

The men wandered back into the lobby. Bill stepped to the doorway of an adjacent parlor and squinted into the darkened room. He entered the room and murmured something I couldn't understand. I figured he was talking to himself in the dark.

Moments later he hurried back into our parlor, aghast.

"There are two women over there going at it!" he blurted. "They're lesbians!"

His friend rushed in behind him. "Bill!" he hissed, raising a finger to his lips.

"That's disgusting!" Bill shouted. "I've never seen anything like it! Have you ever seen such a thing?"

"Yes," Steve said, "we live in San Francisco."

Bill and his friend slumped on the sofa against the opposite wall. There was a cut-out window in the wall, and the two women on the other side could hear every word spoken. Marge and Deena were American exchange students studying in France. They had stayed at the hotel the previous five nights.

"It's disgusting!" Bill growled. His friend tried to change the subject, but Bill kept returning to the "lesbians" and how "disgusting" they were. The rest of us ignored the lout and resumed our conversation.

Bill and his friend finally got up to go to bed. But instead of heading upstairs, Bill strode toward the darkened parlor.

"Bill! Bill! Bill!" his friend said, grabbing him. But Bill shook him off and entered the other parlor.

"Can I join you?" he said. His creepy tone suggested he didn't mean for a chat.

Deena burst from the room in tears and rushed upstairs.

"How do you do what you do?" we heard Bill ask Marge. "I've never seen anything like it."

Marge didn't answer.

I thought it might be time to intervene, but paused when I heard Bill say softly, "Have I upset you? Have I embarrassed you?"

"No, you're embarrassing yourself," Marge said sternly. "You should go to bed."

Bill exited the room and slinked upstairs.

After Bill's door closed, Marge climbed the stairs to the room she shared with Deena.

Marge joined us in the parlor a while later with a glass of red wine and a bottle. Visibly shaken, she gulped down the wine and poured herself another glass. She and Deena had worried about how their sexuality might be received in Morocco, where gay rights aren't protected. But they never dreamed a fellow Western tourist would attack them. Neither of them had ever encountered a bigot who had openly acted on his prejudices.

Deena came back downstairs, and Marge gave her the wing chair. Steve stood and offered his place on the couch to Marge. I tossed another log on the fire.

Marge and Deena attended colleges only five minutes apart in Massachusetts, but they had not met until Paris. Marge planned to attend law school and become an environmental lawyer. Deena hoped to get her teaching credential and work in an inner-city school.

Bill lumbered back downstairs and leaned against the keyhole doorway of the parlor. His hair was mussed, as if he'd already gotten in bed. The six of us ignored him and carried on with our chat. He left without a word.

He returned and again stood in the doorway. None of us made eye contact with him, and again he went back to his room.

When he came back a third time, he again stood in the doorway. He breathed heavily as we froze him out. He took a few tentative steps inside the parlor and stopped next to Deena. He placed his hands in his pockets and leaned down to her.

"I'm sorry," he said.

"I accept your apology," Deena said.

"I'm sorry but I've never in my life seen anything like that."

"I accept your apology."

"Oh, I'm not apologizing," Bill said, flashing a wicked grin. "Where are you from?"

"Washington, D.C.," Deena said.

Bill turned to Marge. "And you? Where are you from?"

"Connecticut," Marge said.

"Where?"

"Connecticut."

"Where?"

"Near New York."

"New York," Bill said, nodding with recognition. "And you're...*friends?*"

"We're traveling together," Marge said.

Gabriela turned to Marge and said, "What kind of dog do you have?" Steve fiddled with his camera equipment, and the rest of us chatted and pretended Bill wasn't there.

Bill wouldn't take the hint. He hovered over Deena, breathing loudly. Deena shrank deeper into her chair.

Andrea's jaw set as she shot Bill a look. "Can you please leave?" she said. "You're making her feel uncomfortable."

Bill leaned into Deena's chair and ogled her through angry, bloodshot eyes.

Marge came off the couch and maneuvered around the table. Deena took Marge's place on the couch. Marge stood toe to toe with Bill, who towered over her. Bill pulled his hands from his pockets.

"Really?" Marge said. "You're going to hit an American woman?"

"I'm a Scottish man!" Bill thundered.

Steve moved toward Bill.

"Come on, this is a small hotel," Steve said. "You're invading our space."

"I'm invading *your* space," Bill said.

"Leave."

"You leave."

"We're on vacation," Steve said.

"*I'm* on vacation," Bill said.

"You're pissing me off," Steve said.

The night watchman entered the parlor. He was a slight, middle-aged man who spoke little English.

"Please," he said to Bill, "please."

The night watchman gently grabbed Bill's elbow and tried to nudge him from the room. "Please," he said, calmly.

Steve grabbed Bill's other arm and tried to help the night watchman. Bill thrashed free of both of them.

The night watchman pulled a cellphone from his pocket. He held it up to Bill and said, "Police."

Bill snickered.

Deena leapt from the sofa and shouted, "Go to bed! You can't treat people this way!" She headed toward Bill.

"It's okay," I said to Deena. "The police will be here soon. Let them handle it."

The night watchman entered a number on his cellphone.

I said to Bill, "Do you really want to spend your holiday in a Moroccan jail?"

Bill assessed the room, eyes darting. He chuckled, shook his head and stalked upstairs.

The night watchman returned the phone to his pocket.

Moments later Deena said she couldn't remember if she had locked their room. Bill had to walk by it on the way to his. I told her I'd check.

I tried the door of Deena and Marge's room. It was locked. I realized I was still holding the fireplace bellows, and I wondered what I'd intended to do with them.

There was a commotion on the floor above me. I hadn't noticed that Steve had followed Bill upstairs.

"If you come out of that room, I'll kill you!" Steve yelled.

When I returned to the parlor, all four women were squeezed together on the red sofa, crying.

Gabriela clutched her stomach. "I can't believe how much this upset me," she said. "I'm in tears."

"Me, too," Andrea said.

In the morning, Bill trudged downstairs and crossed the lobby, head down. He buttonholed the hotel owner. I overheard him say the bed in his room had given him a backache and he and his friend would need to check out a day early. They asked for a taxi and left without eating breakfast.

I recalled the old expression, "Live and let live." I'd heard it my whole life but never gave it much thought. Now it made perfect sense. *Live and let live.* Was there any reason not to?

I regretted not telling Bill to live and let live. Maybe next time.

BOOM-BOOM

On a muggy afternoon in Colombo, Sri Lanka, I shuffled down a crowded sidewalk along Galle Road. My destination was the Galle Face Hotel, the grand colonial hotel where I was staying. As I passed a young man, he glanced down at my feet and said, "I like your shoes!"

I had to look because I couldn't immediately recall which shoes I was wearing. They were an older pair of Merrell hiking shoes, now worn and dirty. They'd already carried me through a three-month tour of Southeast Asia the previous year, and if I had been closer to the end of this particular journey, I may have given them to the man. They were brown, with orange accents. I bought them because they fit well and were on sale. But they were ugly. Still, there was no reason to be rude, so I smiled at the fellow and said, "Thank you."

"Where did you get them?"

"The U.S."

He looked puzzled, then his face brightened with recognition. "Ah, *America*," he said.

Whenever someone asks where I'm from, I say, "the United States" or "the U.S." Most people in the world know what that means. Not most Sri Lankans. Typically, they appear momentarily confused, like this man, then smile and intone,

"Ah, *America*." They pronounce it in a way that makes it sound like it's more than a nation, rather that it's an idea or state of mind, and I suppose that some days it is.

The man lifted one foot, gestured to his shoes and said, "I got mine in Dubai." They were a pair of clunky, black loafers.

"Nice," I lied.

We continued along. Great breakers from the Indian Ocean slammed into the seawall on our left. The sky was unsettled. It was the tail end of the monsoon season and rain was looming.

The young man wore a white collared shirt and dark jeans. His English was quite good, and there was an earnest air about him. He said his name was Kunmara. He worked as a "stock boy" in a supermarket in Dubai. He lived with many other Sri Lankan workers in a bunkroom in the back of the store. Once a year, he returned to Sri Lanka from the Middle East for a two-week visit. This year he was home for four weeks because he was getting married. His fiancée was a "good girl," he said, from the sacred city of Kandy, in the hill country. Like so many others in this predominantly Buddhist country, theirs was an arranged marriage. I asked if his new bride would return with him to Dubai. No, he said, she'd remain in Sri Lanka, and the newlyweds wouldn't see each other again until the following year. I felt sorry for Kunmara, but he was so eager and excited about his impending nuptials, I kept that to myself.

"Today, you are very lucky, sir!" Kunmara said.

"Yeah, why's that?"

"The Buddhist festival." He pointed southeast. I knew that the Gangaramaya Temple, one of the most important Buddhist temples in the country, was somewhere in that direction. "I'm going there now," Kunmara said. "Do you want to come?"

We were nearly to my hotel. I was tired. I had already been sightseeing for most of the day, and my initial thought was to decline Kunmara's invitation. But it was my second day in Sri Lanka and I had interacted only with hotel staff, waiters and tuk-tuk drivers. It seemed silly to pass up the chance to attend a cultural event with a true local from outside the tourist industry. These genuine encounters are so rare. So I agreed.

As soon as I said yes, Kunmara darted out into the street. He raised an arm to halt traffic. He strode confidently as a river of cars, buses, trucks, taxis and tuk-tuks stopped, or at least slowed. Halfway across, he turned and beckoned me to follow, and I did.

We reached the other side and headed down a broad, busy boulevard that flanked a lime-green canal. A helicopter zoomed by overhead. Kunmara looked up. "That is our president," he said. "He is going to the festival." Wow, what luck, I thought. Kunmara walked faster, and I hustled to keep pace.

I'm a brisk walker, but I soon fell behind. Kunmara was practically running, eager to reach the temple before the president left. It was hot, and my pants stuck to my sweaty legs. I noticed the endless parade of empty tuk-tuks that sputtered past. I had already ridden in a couple that morning. They were convenient and cheap. I don't know why I didn't suggest we hire one. I just didn't. Instead, I called to Kunmara.

"How much further?" I said.

He stopped and turned. Seeing I was tuckered, he offered a sympathetic smile. "We can take a tuk-tuk the rest of the way," he said. I exhaled with relief. Kunmara hailed a tuk-tuk, and we climbed in back.

On the ride to the temple, Kunmara filled me in on the details of his wedding. It was to be held at the Queen's Hotel, in Kandy. I recognized the name, as I was holding a reservation for that hotel for the following week. I wondered whether I'd be there at the same time. Kunmara said the reception would start early in the morning and last all day. He grew more animated as he described the festivities. There would be food and drink and music and dancing and much laughter.

"Then at four o'clock, I have boom-boom," he said excitedly.

"Boom-boom?" I asked.

"Boom-boom," he repeated, this time with a vulgar gesture.

"Oh," I said, "boom-boom."

His mother would play a role in the consummation of the marriage. Not in the actual act, but afterwards.

"At four-thirty, she will enter the room and take the sheets," Kunmara said. "If there is blood, there is marriage. No blood, divorce." He clapped his hands once to demonstrate how swift and sure annulment would come if his bride were deemed unchaste.

I asked whether men in his culture were also expected to be virgins on their wedding day. Kunmara snickered, then said something in Sinhalese to the tuk-tuk driver. Both men hee-hawed wildly.

Kunmara said his mother would take some of his bride's vaginal blood and mix it with food to be served at the wedding feast. Before I could ask him more about this custom, we had arrived at the temple. I started to pay the tuk-tuk driver. Kunmara stopped me and said the driver would wait for us.

We removed our shoes and left them in the cubbyholes outside the temple. A small elephant, two of its legs shackled in chains, stood forlornly at the entrance. Inside, we stopped in front of a bejeweled Buddha statue behind a glass case. Kunmara told me the significance of this statue, but he spoke rapidly, and I couldn't understand. He hastily moved on to another statue, mumbled a few words of explanation, then headed for another Buddha. The next few minutes were a whirl of Buddhas and brief, incomprehensible stories. This was fine by me. I had visited a slew of Buddhist temples in recent years, and I wasn't interested in some long, drawn-out tour. I was here to see the festival. But as my eyes adjusted to the light, I saw only a few monks and tourists milling about.

"Where's the festival?" I said to Kunmara.

"It is here," he said. "Every day there is festival here." He launched into another summary of another statue.

"And the president?" I asked. "Where's he?"

"He is gone already," Kunmara said, looking down.

Kunmara surely sensed my suspicion. He suggested we leave, and I agreed. We had spent all of three minutes inside the temple.

We collected our shoes. The tuk-tuk driver still waited at the curb. We climbed inside and drove off.

"Okay," Kunmara said, "now I have to stop at a jewelry store. I'm going to buy my bride a surprise for our wedding day."

So there it was, at last. The scam revealed. The word "jewelry" hung there on the humid air.

It's easy to spot most touts. They're the "friendly" locals stepping in your path, asking where you're from and how long you're visiting their country. A sad truth about travel in poorer, developing nations is that nearly everyone who approaches you on the street is a tout. They prey on the traveler's desire for cultural exchange—and soon your new "friend" is steering you to a gem dealer in India or a rug merchant in Morocco or a batik shop in Indonesia. Over the years, I've learned to ignore suspected touts, to not even return their greetings. That may sound mean, but it saves both parties a lot of time and grief.

But Kunmara was running the long con. Those touts are much harder to spot. It had been a dozen years since I'd fallen for such a ruse, and Kunmara was good at his trade. He hadn't directly approached me; he had instead allowed me to catch up to him on the sidewalk, making our encounter seem organic. And that bit about the president in the helicopter, which hooked me, displayed a true nimbleness. (I later learned that at that moment, Sri Lankan President Mahinda Rajapaksa was attending an economic summit in Kuwait.)

Kunmara's failing, however, was he had just wasted a chunk of his day on the one tourist who never buys anything. That's right, whenever I travel, I return home empty-handed. Customs agents give me sideways glances when I affirm I have nothing to declare; some will search my backpack, looking disappointed when all they turn up is a load of dirty laundry. The truth is, travel costs money, and I prefer to spend it collecting experiences rather than souvenirs. If I ever did develop a hankering for "precious" stones, I'd certainly never enlist the aid of a tout.

"I have absolutely no interest in going to a jewelry store," I said to Kunmara.

"Not even to get something for your wife?"

"I'm going back to my hotel now. Can I drop you somewhere?"

"But it's on the way," he said.

"I don't care. I'm going to my hotel. Do you want me to drop you somewhere or not?"

Kunmara told the tuk-tuk driver to go to the Galle Face Hotel. The rest of the ride was a little uncomfortable as Kunmara pouted the whole way. I wondered whether anything he told me was true: his job in Dubai, his wedding, even his name.

When we reached Galle Road, the tuk-tuk driver parked across the street from my hotel. That was odd. Plus, it would be a real hassle crossing the congested street without Kunmara running interference.

I reached into my pocket for some rupees to pay the driver. "I'll get the tuk-tuk," I said to Kunmara. "How much is it?"

Kunmara spoke to the driver in Sinhalese and translated for me.

"Twenty-eight hundred," he said.

I figured Kunmara had misspoken and meant to say, "two-eighty." The going fare for a five-minute tuk-tuk ride was one hundred rupees. (This was the tourist rate; locals paid much less.) We had taken two five-minute tuk-tuk rides. That should cost two hundred. Plus an extra eighty for the few minutes the driver waited outside the temple. So, two hundred eighty rupees, while more than generous, sounded about right. Not twenty-eight hundred.

"What?" I said to Kunmara.

"Twenty-eight hundred," he said. "Two thousand eight hundred." He reached into his pocket and removed a wad of rupees. "Each," he said. "I pay, too."

"You're kidding!"

"No," he said. "It's a good price."

As I watched Kunmara peel off several rupee notes and hand them to the driver, the depth of the deception finally hit me. I wasn't facing one con man, but two. These guys were a team. The tuk-tuk driver had been following us from the start, waiting for Kunmara to wear me out walking and signal him to zoom in and pick us up. It didn't occur to me to establish the fare before entering the tuk-tuk—as I had on every other ride in Colombo—because I was in the company of a trusted local who was taking me to see the festival. I now realized this is where we were headed all along: a tuk-tuk shakedown for roughly fourteen times the customary fare. The commission from the jewelry store, if I had agreed to go, would've been a bonus.

I shook with anger and fear. I was mad at these two, but I was mostly mad at myself for getting so thoroughly duped. I don't know why, but I take these things personally. I was also worried for my safety. I was in a cramped tuk-tuk with two young men who were essentially trying to rob me. I wondered if I could extricate my long-limbed body from the tiny vehicle without getting grabbed. Unless the pair showed me a gun or a knife, I wasn't about to hand over anything close to 2,800 rupees.

I jumped from the tuk-tuk, and the driver bounded behind me onto the sidewalk.

"Twenty-eight hundred is too much," I said.

"How much you pay?" the driver said, speaking English for the first time since I'd met him. Unlike the typical slightly built Sri Lankan male, this dude was burly. And while I may have stood taller, he was half my age.

"I only paid one hundred for much longer rides," I said.

"No, no," he said, shaking his thick head.

I glanced over at Kunmara, who sat in the back of the tuk-tuk, feigning ignorance.

"How much you pay?" the driver said. He was in my face. "You pay two thousand."

"Two thousand?" I said. "I paid two thousand for a three-hour ride in an air conditioned taxi from the airport."

His face soured. "How can you stay in expensive hotel and not pay tuk-tuk man?"

"I'll pay you the correct fare."

"You pay sixteen hundred."

"Look, you gave me two short rides," I said. "I'll pay you two hundred."

"You shouldn't get in tuk-tuk if you can't pay," he yelled.

I yelled, "You shouldn't be dishonest and steal from tourists."

I noticed Kunmara step out of the tuk-tuk and slink down the sidewalk.

The driver changed tack. He pulled a fistful of rupees from his pocket. "Okay, you no pay me," he said. "I pay you. How much you want?"

I said, "Twenty-eight hundred."

The driver leaned in. I thought he might hit me. "Okay," he said, "you pay me two hundred."

As I pulled some bills from my pocket, the driver told me I'd never get another tuk-tuk ride in Sri Lanka. "You have to walk everywhere you go." He took a couple mopey steps down the sidewalk to pantomime my future transportation woes. He turned back, and as I prepared to hand over the two hundred rupees, he said, "Give me fifty more."

"No!" I returned all the cash to my pocket, wondering why I had to give even a single rupee to these thieves. How many frightened tourists had they already fleeced? "I'm giving you nothing!"

His jaw clenched. He looked up and down the street and back at me. "Go!" he snapped, waving me off.

"You go," I said.

"This is my Sri Lanka!" he raged. "You go, I stay!"

I didn't move.

It started to pour, and we stood there glaring at each other in the rain.

The driver finally shook his head, returned to his tuk-tuk and drove off.

Thirty or so yards down Galle Road, the tuk-tuk pulled to the curb and stopped. Kunmara, no longer obliged to pretend he didn't know his cohort, ducked out from under an awning and stepped toward the tuk-tuk. Sheets of rain fell and there was a clap of thunder. I called to Kunmara and he looked back.

I yelled, "No boom-boom for you!"

THE BIRTHDAY PARTY

At the Nagyatád Refugee Camp in Hungary, near the Croatian border, I visited with Fata, a skinny blond girl with eyes like brown yo-yos. She, her sister and mother had fled war-torn Bosnia fourteen months earlier. They were among some two thousand refugees living at the converted army base. They shared a room with two other Muslim families. Their fifteen beds were crammed into a cement space the size of a single-car garage. Laundry hung from clotheslines over the bunks. They shared the floor's lone bathroom with another 120 refugees. Fata supposed her father and brother were still fighting the Serbs in Bosnia—or dead.

It was Fata's sixteenth birthday. She offered me a slice of white sheet cake from a plate resting near a copy of the Koran. She had made her own birthday card and taped it to the wall above her bed between posters of Madonna and New Kids on the Block. The crayon drawing depicted a jagged heart ripped in two and dripping red tears. Beneath the broken heart, Fata had scrawled a peace sign and the message, "Life is shit."

In another of the camp's drab brown barracks, a teenaged boy named Musa invited me into his room with a sweep of his hand.

"Welcome to my home," he said, gesturing to one of the dozen bunks lining the bare concrete wall.

Four beds down, a ninety-year-old man lay on his back, staring at the ceiling.

Musa had arrived alone at the camp only the day before. He was a bright-faced handsome kid who grinned a lot, though I wasn't sure why.

"My house in Sarajevo, it fall," he said in broken English. "Big grenade."

His father died in the blast. Musa and the rest of the family ran from the building. He watched in horror as Serb forces caught and killed his mother and older brother. He drew a finger across his throat to show how. "Knife," he said, his lower lip trembling. As he fled the city, he kept slipping on blood in the streets. "No go back Bosnia. It's nothing."

Musa pulled a cardboard box from under his bed. It contained a roll of toilet paper, a coverless paperback and a change of underwear. At the bottom of the box was a pair of padded pants he used in Sarajevo when he practiced his passion, kickboxing. He wore the remainder of his belongings—an old scuffed pair of brown shoes (no socks), red jeans with a belt that wrapped around his waist nearly twice, and a T-shirt that read, "U.S.A."

"This is it," he said, "this is my life." He said it over and over, laughing as if he couldn't believe it himself. "This is my life."

The entire camp filed into the cafeteria for the usual nightly fare: baloney, rolls and tea. The photographer I worked with had a car. I asked Musa if he'd rather eat with us in town, and he quickly agreed.

Concrete walls and barbed wire surrounded the camp, and refugees were not allowed out. So we hid Musa under a blanket in the back seat and drove past the guards at the gate.

We found a pizzeria in Nagyatád and ordered a pie. Over dinner, Musa showed me a page torn from an address book. It listed the names and phone numbers of three people from Italy, Sweden and the Netherlands. They were tourists Musa had met during his days as a waiter in Sarajevo. He hoped one of them would sponsor him and get him a visa.

I knew I had crossed a line when I busted Musa out of the camp for the evening. My job was to be an objective, detached journalist—not a participant in the story. I thought I was being decent. I thought that buying Musa dinner in town might lift his spirits. But I now saw my gesture as hollow and pathetic. A tragic tale in return for a few slices of pizza. It wasn't a fair exchange. Musa smiled as he ate his pizza. I felt like a ghoul. Musa told me again and again how much he enjoyed the pizza. The more he enjoyed it, the more ghoulish I felt.

When we returned to the camp, Fata's birthday party was in full swing in a corner room of Building 4. Inflated condoms, substituting for balloons, hung from the ceiling. The walls were now a pastel fresco of peace symbols, palm trees and sunsets. "Peace," the wall read. "Make Love, Not War." And: "The Doors, Deep Purple, Led Zeppelin." The place was dubbed the International Room because the young people who gathered there represented the ethnic makeup of the former Yugoslavia: Serbs, Muslims, Croats, Hungarians, as well as various mixtures. Their relatives were killing each other back home, explained a boy named Elvis, but in this room they were all friends.

The youngsters sat on bunks and listened to a guy play an old Bo Diddley tune on a borrowed guitar and harmonica. "Before you accuse me, take a look at yourself," sang Rosandro, who was part Serb, part Muslim and part Italian. Before the war, the twenty-four-year-old fronted an R&B band in Bosnia called the Gillettes, named after the razor company. He had lost track of the rest of his band. "Maybe my guitar man now take gun," he said. "Maybe he dead."

I looked around for Fata and found her passed out on a bed in the corner. Someone said she drank a whole bottle of homemade brandy, a concoction that tastes like gasoline. Someone else said Fata also took some pills. Girls splashed water on her face and yanked on her arms. But the birthday girl wouldn't wake up. The music stopped and the authorities were summoned. An ambulance came and carried Fata to the town hospital. The next day, after she had recovered, she was moved into the mental ward.

RAMBO IN YUMA

I was sitting in a bar in Yuma, Arizona, when Sylvester Stallone rolled into town in a luxury RV to battle the Russians. The nearby desert served as Soviet-occupied Afghanistan for the finale of *Rambo III*. Two hundred Marines from the local air station played Red Army soldiers, and a group of Los Angeles-based Afghani immigrants stood in for the freedom fighters.

The shoot drew cowboys from as far away as Montana seeking work as extra horsemen. One of the buckaroos bought me a beer.

"We hear they got a bunch of no-ridin', round-butted dinks on this picture," he said.

The next afternoon, Sly swaggered from his RV to a commissary tent for the photo op. A manservant followed him, running his fingers through the star's hair, setting the curls just right.

"Little windy out there," Stallone grunted as the manservant primped.

The manservant stepped away, then rushed back in for more grooming. He stepped away again, then returned for some fluffing.

Stallone asked somebody to close the tent flap, and three lackeys lunged for it.

The manservant adjusted a few more curls and stepped away.

Stallone ran his fingers through his hair, then nodded.

Cameras clicked and lights flashed.

"It's an incredible responsibility doing this film when that bloodletting is going on," Sly proclaimed.

Then he walked out of the tent and the wind messed up his hair.

Ali Sadiqyar, an extra who fought the Soviets in his homeland for six months, called the movie unbelievable.

"One person fighting against the whole army?" he said, and laughed.

Filming was canceled one day because Stallone was cold, Sadiqyar said. "If he can't come out in cold weather, how can he fight the Russians?"

I left the set and drove downtown. On the main drag, a man in a Jack Daniels baseball hat worked under the hood of a car. He pointed a wrench at the granite building across the street.

"That's the Yuma County Jail, bud," he told me. "I did a little time in there."

The man ducked back under the hood of the car. He said he was replacing the timing chain and gear. He said the car belonged to the bail bondsman who posted his bail.

"The kid didn't have diapers," he explained. "Me and another guy, we broke into a house and stole a TV and jewelry and shit. This is a real depressed area. Lot of people going to jail here, bud."

The man gave the wrench a hard turn. He said he didn't plan to see *Rambo III* when it came out. Too many mouths to feed.

"My daughter, she's in Flagstaff with her grandmother," he said. "Her mother got killed three months ago."

He labored to get at the timing chain and gear.

"Some guy shot her, up in Laughlin," he said. "I didn't care for her too much, but she didn't deserve that. The guy shot her in the head and left her in the desert. Then he went down to Florida and killed another woman there and got caught."

The man leaned back from under the hood and pointed the wrench at an exposed part of the engine.

"That's your timing chain and gear, bud."

TRANSITS

"I heard an airplane passing overhead. I wished I was on it."
—Charles Bukowski

FINAL APPROACH

The final approach to Paro, Bhutan, is the most exhilarating in commercial aviation.

After you wave to Mount Everest out the window, the captain makes the following announcement:

"For those who are flying into Paro for the first time, do not be alarmed by how close the plane comes to the landscape."

The Drukair Airbus A319 then goes into a dive as the pilot finds the critical crease in the Himalayas.

You now feel like you're flying inside a video game with a teenager at the joystick. You look across the aisle at the two Bhutanese women, who only moments earlier were having a laugh over a hunk of yak cheese. One now prays fervently while the other is already braced for impact. As the plane plummets and banks sickeningly, you spot the runway below. It looks unnatural, like a football field wedged at a cockamamie angle inside a baseball stadium.

Plunging faster, the plane now enters a narrow, twisting ravine and negotiates a series of overlapping ridgelines. Indeed, the "landscape" looks close—like maybe seven inches away. At times, it seems like the plane is flying at a 180-degree-angle— one wing pointing to the sky, the other to the ground. You imagine the captain saying to the co-pilot, "What the heck, we're halfway there, let's go for the full barrel roll."

As the plane scrapes by the last ridge, you can see the nervous smiles of people inside their houses. The ridge can't be cleared in a straight line with the runway, so there is a final violent lurch to the left seconds before the wheels slam the tarmac. But you're not clapping yet. A mountain looms at the end of the abbreviated runway. The pilot puts everything he's got into the brakes and the reverse thrusters as your face hurtles toward the seat back in front of you.

When at last the plane comes to a stop and you descend the stairway, you don't kiss the ground—you make love to it.

FIRST FLIGHT

The man in the seat next to me said it was his first flight. He had reserved a window seat for the occasion. But the window seat in our row had no window. I felt bad for the guy. For a while.

He was an engineer from Sri Lanka's roads department, and he was flying to Thailand to learn how to build better roads. He was a small man with a patchy salt-and-pepper beard and a protruding tooth that looked like it wanted to shake hands. Within minutes, he had wrangled my phone number and email address from me and entered them into his ancient cellphone. I told him he needed to turn off his phone because we were taking off, but he left it on.

I inserted the jack from my earbuds into the video screen in the seat back in front of me. I found Terrence Malick's *Days of Heaven* and fast-forwarded to the part where I'd fallen asleep during an earlier flight. My seatmate was perplexed by the video-on-demand function, so I showed him how to touch his screen to make a selection. He settled on the channel that shows real-time flight information, including altitude, airspeed and maps. The screen displayed the route of our three-hour flight from Colombo to Bangkok. The man whipped out a camera and snapped a photo of the screen.

A minute later, I realized the man was speaking to me. I removed one of my earbuds so I could hear him. He had unwrapped the airline's headphones and was wondering what to do with the plastic bag.

"No bin?" he said.

I told him to stuff the bag in the seat back pouch and returned my attention to the movie.

Soon he was again talking to me and I removed an earbud. He nodded in the direction of the beverage cart.

"You have drinks?" he said.

The beverage cart was in the front of the cabin, about twenty rows away.

"Eventually," I said.

The man grinned, and there was that tooth again.

Somewhere over the Bay of Bengal, we ran into severe turbulence. The captain came on the PA system and told the flight crew to take their seats. Two flight attendants returned the beverage cart to the galley.

The man was talking again, so I pulled out an earbud.

"No have drinks?" he said.

I explained the safety issue, but I don't think he understood.

Days of Heaven had reached the part where the barnstormers fly over Sam Shepard's farm. So while the plane I was on dipped and rocked, I watched film of another plane bouncing through the sky. The effect was unsettling, and my pesky neighbor only added to my anxiety.

When the beverage service resumed a half hour later, I ordered a glass of white wine. The Sri Lankan Airlines flight attendant didn't give the man next to me a choice. "Would you like some orange juice?" she said. Most Sri Lankans are Buddhists, and she must have assumed he didn't drink. When he asked for wine, she poured him a glass and set it before him with a look of disdain.

The man downed his wine in three large gulps. Then he was on his feet and moving toward the aisle. I had no time to stand or even unbuckle my seat belt. The man climbed over my legs, dislodging my earbuds cord from the screen as he passed. I guess he really had to go.

He hustled up the aisle toward the bathrooms. He tried one door but it wouldn't open. Good thing, too, because he was pulling on the handle of the emergency door. He looked back at me. I motioned toward the bank of lavatories in the middle of the plane. He may have thought I was instructing him how to work the emergency door handle because he kept struggling with it. He shook his head and threw his hands up and returned to his seat.

"It's engaged," he said.

I watched my movie. Richard Gere had killed Sam Shepard and now a posse tracked him with dogs. From the corner of my eye, I caught a flash of yellow. I turned and saw that the man next to me had found the life vest under his seat and removed it from its pouch. He fiddled with the light and whistle. Then he pulled the cord, and the vest inflated with a suddenness that surprised us both.

A flight attendant rushed up. She spoke sternly to the man in their language and snatched the vest from him. He looked like a scolded child.

On my screen, the posse caught up to Richard Gere and gunned him down in the river. I wondered what would become of Brooke Adams and the girl. I was about to find out when I heard the muffled sounds of my neighbor trying to communicate with me yet again.

I yanked out both earbuds this time.

"What?" I said. "I couldn't hear you."

"I was saying, I like to chat."

And so we did.

WIDESPREAD PANIC

My flight from La Ceiba, on the mainland of Honduras, to Útila, one of the Bay Islands, cost nine dollars and seventy-five cents. I had a boarding pass, but it didn't guarantee me a seat on the plane. None of the other passengers had boarding passes. They all appeared to be hitchhikers who knew the pilots.

At departure time, which varied wildly from day to day, it was every *hombre* for himself. When the inbound flight landed, everyone rushed the plane, clutching baggage and infants and animals, as the propellers still turned.

I scampered aboard and shared a bench seat built for two with a woman and her three children. Her husband sat across the aisle, holding a pig. There were no announcements about seat belts and emergency exits, and as we made our final approach into Útila Airport and its single dirt runway, I glimpsed one of the pilots hurriedly paging through what I feared was a flight instruction manual.

I checked into a basic, but colorful, room at Blueberry Hill, then sampled the tropical fare at Selley's, where the immense cook insisted you retrieve your own beers from her kitchen refrigerator. Many of the island's 2,500 residents are Garifuna, descendants of shipwrecked African slaves. Most of the local

Anglo population are the progeny of pirates. Hardly anybody speaks Spanish. The favored tongue is an often difficult-to-comprehend, yet melodic, Caribbean English.

At the legendary Bucket of Blood, a sagging structure once named by *Esquire* magazine as one of the world's top ten bars, inebriated men with rheumy eyes played dominos. They slammed the bones down hard on the tables, as if engaged in aerobic exercise.

I visited with the longtime proprietor, Mr. Clifford, aged seventy-six and sporting a L.A. Dodgers baseball cap. His seventeen-year-old wife was pregnant with her third child, his fourteenth. Caribbean music blared from massive speakers. Some young backpacker interrupted us. She pressed a cassette tape into Mr. Clifford's hand and asked him to play it, and he obliged. It was music from the American jam band Widespread Panic. At least the song was "Coconut," lending a patina of authenticity.

In the ensuing years, waves of scuba-diving backpackers would inundate the island, drawn by its proximity to the Mesoamerican Barrier Reef, the largest coral reef in the Western Hemisphere. They'd bring their music to the Bucket of Blood—pop, disco, electronica, rap, techno—and Mr. Clifford would oblige them, until his place lost all its local funky flavor. Things would not work out well for Mr. Clifford, either. A petty thief from the mainland, an occasional domino partner of Mr. Clifford's, robbed him on his way to work, slit his throat, and left him to die in the brush.

There wasn't a terminal at the airport, so when it was time to fly back, I wasn't surprised to learn the airline ticket office was in a local bar. ("What'll it be, *mon*?" "Uh, a cold beer, a shot of rum and a one-way ticket to La Ceiba, please.") Out on the dirt runway, the airport commissioner, who doubled as the customs agent, greeted us. I recognized him as one of the drunken domino players from the Bucket of Blood. He looked horribly hungover, and I hoped he hadn't been partying with the pilots.

"If any of you are carrying drugs, you have to share them with me," he said.

He caught me staring at the orange windsock, which looked like it might rip from the pole.

"There's a good wind today," he said to me. "You should make it to the mainland quick, *mon*—if you don't flip."

TSUNAMI TRAIN

The Sri Lankan passenger train named the Rajarata Rajina (Queen of the Land of Kings) will never be confused for the Orient Express. Its cars are squalid, its seats worn and grimy, its dining service nonexistent. But it does offer terrific value. I was traveling about three hours—from Colombo, the country's largest city, to Galle, a fortified city on the southwestern tip of the island nation. My ticket cost 180 rupees, the equivalent of $1.38.

The train was scheduled to depart the Fort Railway Station at ten-thirty in the morning. Even though Sri Lanka's trains are notoriously tardy, I stood on the platform a half hour early. I hoped to snag a window seat on the right side of the unreserved southbound train. The coastal line skirts the Indian Ocean, and those lucky enough to land in the proper seats are treated to some glorious views. But my early arrival did me no good. When the train pulled into the station, passengers rushed the doorways and I found myself at the back of the pack. Fortunately, most people held tickets for the third-class cars. When I reached the second-class car, all the window seats were taken, but there remained one aisle seat on the side of the train that would face the sea. I hoisted my backpack onto the overhead luggage rack and plopped down next to a balding, middle-aged man.

We were a few minutes outside the congested city when I glimpsed the turquoise water, tan sand and swaying coconut palms. Fishermen paired off alongside the tracks, untangling and organizing their nets while boys bounded over the rocks with fishing poles in hand. A young couple sat beneath a black umbrella that warded off the tropical sun. Every window on the train was open, and at times we came so close to the sea that crashing waves sent mist and flecks of foam into our car.

The man next to me was a train security officer. He used to enforce the smoking ban onboard and arrest fare cheats and vandals, but these days he worked a desk job in Matara, at the end of the line. Twice a week, he commuted seven hours from his home in Kandy because he didn't want to uproot his family. He said he never tired of the view out the window and after a while he offered to trade seats. "We switch a little bit, then we switch back," he said. Ten minutes later, I tried to give him back his seat, but he told me to stay put, and I did, all the way to Galle.

The train veered inland and passed behind homes wedged between the tracks and the ocean. Some were tidy and bright, but most were shacks, with corrugated tin roofs and listing walls of splintered scrap wood.

The land was lush and green, with a riot of wildflowers. A shirtless old man, bronzed and beatific, stared into my eyes as we chugged by. A sari-clad woman bathed in a lagoon. Two men carried a mattress across the tracks as a small boy urinated nearby. Laundry was set out to dry on the ground. Dogs dozed and cows grazed. Surveyors measured a parcel that would become a new beach resort. (The decades-long civil war was recently over and tourism had exploded.) I followed the flight of a bird a shade of blue I had never seen. When it landed atop a mango tree, I spotted a man lounging in a crook of the tree, reading a newspaper.

At Maggona station, a goat stood on the platform, munching on an encroaching shrub, and a passenger boarded carrying six cardboard boxes of chirping chicks.

South of Ambalangoda, we returned to the coast, and I noticed something about the houses. They were of low quality, like the ones farther north, but they all looked new. Then came a succession of graves laid out along the tracks, mere steps from the sea. And their markers, like the houses, all appeared to be of the same recent age.

"Tsunami people," my seatmate said.

More than 35,000 Sri Lankans perished in the 2004 tsunami, the second-highest death toll among the fifteen nations affected. Seventeen hundred of the victims were killed when a train on this line was swept away by a wall of water. I knew these facts before I arrived. What I didn't know was that most of Sri Lanka's victims were women. My seatmate explained why: When the first wave hit, it literally stripped the clothes from people's bodies, he said. Rather than fleeing to higher ground with the naked masses, many women, bound by feelings of modesty and embarrassment, remained in place, covering their breasts with their arms and crouching. Then the second, deadlier, wave burst ashore. The man told me that for many of the women who survived the killer waves, their ordeal was just beginning. In the chaotic aftermath, countless women were raped by their neighbors.

Outside Hikkaduwa we passed the giant Buddha statue on the beach. It stands fifty-four feet tall and faces the ocean. It was built with Japanese donations as a memorial to the victims of the tsunami. The Buddha's right hand is raised, its palm facing outward. I know that in Buddhism, this gesture is called the *Abhaya mudra* and symbolizes fearlessness. But that giant raised hand made me think the Buddha was emphatically commanding the sea, "No more!"

NO MAN'S LAND

The southbound train stopped on the frontier between Hungary and Serbia. There were few passengers on board. Who wanted to tour the Balkans during the war?

I glanced out the window and saw the stampeding horde. Hundreds of men, women and children raced across the wintry fields. As the mob closed in, I wondered why the train didn't try to get away. I looked for an escape route, but it was too late.

A gang of men burst into my compartment. They appeared ragged and desperate. I flinched, but the men ignored me, instead hurrying to stow packages overhead and beneath the seats. Women outside frantically passed infants and bags through the window. There were seats for six, but my compartment swelled with twenty people or more.

I learned the new passengers had ventured to this no man's land to buy goods on the black market. The U.N. had imposed sanctions against Serbia for its role in the Bosnian conflict, crippling its economy. Food, medicine and clothing were now scarce in Belgrade.

A woman wedged into the bench seat next to me. Her face was smudged and tired. She reached into the bag at her feet and pulled out a new pair of shoes. They were shoddy, perhaps cardboard, with a thin layer of crimson velvet. She caressed one of the shoes, stroking the velvet this way and that, then clutched it to her breast like a baby.

The train rolled on. In the crowded compartment, there was little talk. There was only a quiet murmur. Mostly, there was relief.

PASSENGERS

The observation car was at the end of a train that chugged through the hill country of Sri Lanka. I had lucked into seat number forty-four, in the last row, which faced the giant window at the rear. Riding backwards, I gazed out at rolling tea estates hemmed by mountainsides dotted with white Buddhist stupas. The compartment was full except for the empty seat next to me.

The day before, after climbing Little Adam's Peak, I'd checked into a run-down guesthouse in the village of Ella. My room was as bright as a cave, with stained curtains, filthy floor mats and a rotted door that wouldn't stay closed. I didn't spot the crack in the toilet seat until after I sat down and it nipped a sliver of flesh from my hide. Rats scurried between the ceiling and the roof tiles as I tossed and turned on a thin, soiled mattress. I was visited by strange dreams, not nightmares, but unsettling. It was all worth it in the morning, however, when I stepped onto the balcony and gaped at the view. Snow-white clouds clung to the valleys and peaks of the Ella Gap far below and evoked a glacier tumbling down to the sea. I was awake but it looked like a vision. Hours later, after boarding the train, I still felt as if I were traveling through a dream.

As the train clattered and lurched up the mountain, it occasionally slowed to a crawl, and people walking along the tracks passed us. We picked up speed and entered a great curve. I leaned out my side window and saw the engine and the red cars ahead approaching a bridge so fatigued I wondered if it could remain standing another day. On the hillside above stood some tall, slender trees so white they looked like spirits creeping through the darker forest. The conductor, dressed in the white uniform favored by the staff of insane asylums, checked my ticket.

A man with a German accent left his seat and sat down beside me. He said he was from Frankfurt and this was his fourth trip to Sri Lanka. He relayed this as he pointed his video camera out the window at a pair of bleating goats and a few cows grazing at the edge of a half-flooded cricket pitch. Learning I was from California, he volunteered he had twice driven the length of the state. Had he seen Death Valley? I asked. He had, in the summer, when the thermometer topped 120 degrees. The snowpack in the Sierra was so heavy that year, he added, he had to make a wide detour to reach Lake Tahoe. Hearing the name of my boyhood home, I considered what to say next: Had he leaned over Fanny Bridge to watch the fat trout swimming in the Truckee River, say, or ridden a mountain bike down the Flume Trail? But before I could put a question to him, I glanced out the window and saw a small boy, not much taller than the weeds growing between the tracks, running after the train and waving. I wondered whether he was waving at me, or the train in general. Then the kid disappeared, and I realized the train had entered a long, dark tunnel.

Inside the compartment, it was pitch black. It couldn't have been darker had I closed my eyes, and I had the sensation of floating. When the train exited the tunnel and light streamed into the car, I saw that the German tourist was no longer sitting beside me. In his place was an old Sri Lankan gentleman who stared straight ahead out the rear window, blankly, not uttering a word. He was a slight man, with grey hair, a red and gold shirt, and black trousers. He wore no shoes. One of his pant legs had hiked up his calf. His tan skin was segmented by white geometric lines and reminded me of the coat pattern of a giraffe.

The train wended through a succession of tunnels, each longer than the last. During the periods of darkness, a hush fell over the compartment, as if we were all holding our breath. It took many minutes to get through the final tunnel. Nobody said anything. I felt something bump my side. When at last daylight flooded the car, I glanced to my right and found that the old man was asleep, his head resting on my shoulder. In his somnolent state, he looked much younger. My stop was in Nanu Oya, another couple hours down the line. I studied the old fellow's peaceful face. Let him sleep, I thought. Sweet dreams.

ALL ABOARD!

We switched trains in Taiyuan, China, in the northern province of Shanxi. Inside the terminal, Andrea spotted the "soft" (first-class) waiting room. But, no, I had to queue with the proletariat. We joined a mob not witnessed since India, or at least since Black Friday outside Walmart.

They opened the gate three minutes before the train was scheduled to depart. Thousands of passengers rushed the lone ticket-taker. I felt something tug the hem of my shorts. I glanced down and saw a little boy. In the surging press of humanity, there was no room to turn and look for a parent. One could only hope.

On the platform, there ensued a mad dash for the carriages, numbered 1 to 20. Train officials blew their whistles. They shouted and urged us on. We jostled, tripped, lunged and laughed. More shrill whistles pierced the air. We were six carriages short of our car when we heard the telltale hiss and jumped aboard.

We had six "hard" (second-class) cars to negotiate before we could rest. Cars with seats for eighty now held two hundred, three hundred or more.

Andrea prepared to run interference, backpack hoisted overhead. She wanted to give up, but I wouldn't let her.

"The longest journey begins with a single step," I shouted above the din.

Andrea bravely raised a foot, then lowered it in defeat.

"There's room, there's room!" I implored. "Just beyond that old man's knee."

Not all of our steps found the floor, but we reached our car and rode deeper into the Middle Kingdom.

AFRICA

One sunny afternoon in La Jolla, California, I carried a dozen or so ironed shirts from the dry cleaner's to my car at the curb. A woman on the sidewalk stopped me. She looked to be in her seventies, perhaps her eighties. She held a plastic bag of groceries from the Vons across the street. She asked me to help get her groceries home. She said she lived around the corner.

"Sure," I said.

I set my shirts on the seat of my car and closed the door. When I turned around to take the bag of groceries from the woman, she pulled back. She said it was okay, she had it. Why did she need my help? Did she just want me to walk her home?

The woman nodded at my car.

"You can drive me," she said.

I finally saw the metal cane she was leaning on. She took a few faltering steps toward my car, her feet scarcely leaving the ground. Each footfall extended her journey by mere inches. Minutes passed before she reached my car door.

I opened the door for her. I grasped her arm and tried to help her sit down.

She shook me off.

"I'll do it myself," she said. Her words were slurred, like she'd been drinking. "If I don't do it myself, I won't win."

She smiled. Her lipstick was smeared and only one side of her mouth moved.

The woman rested her cane on her wrist and gripped the top of the open door. She braced her other hand against the headrest of the passenger seat. She squatted and struggled to lower herself into the seat. I watched helplessly, worried a passerby might see me not helping an old woman who obviously could use some assistance. The woman squatted deeper, still gripping the door and the headrest. At last she let go and plopped into the seat. She used both hands to lift her legs into the car one at a time.

I had a little Fiat convertible with a busted passenger seat. When the woman leaned back, the seat didn't stop reclining until her legs were in the air and she faced the sky. She reminded me of a geriatric astronaut. We drove the half block to her place with my shirts on her lap.

The woman asked what I did for a living. When I told her I was a journalist, she brightened. She used to be a writer, she said. She wrote for various women's magazines and traveled the world. About fifteen years ago, she had a stroke and retired.

She lived at a seniors-only apartment building, one of the few high-rises in La Jolla. It blocked the view of the ocean and I'd always ignored it. But now there I was, pulling into the driveway.

The woman told me to drive down the ramp to the underground garage. She said to stop in front of the entrance. As close as we were to the door, I knew it would take forever for her to shuffle to it by herself. I considered turning the car around to get the passenger door closer to the entrance. But it was too late—she was already straining to rise from the seat.

I hurried around to her door, but again she refused my help.

"If I don't do it myself, I won't win," she said.

And again that crooked smile.

She let me carry her groceries. I figured I'd hand them to her at the entrance and be on my way. But when we reached the door and I tried to hand her the bag, she asked if I'd carry it up to her apartment. I hesitated. Before I could answer, her back was to me, and her cane already through the door.

A bank of elevators stood across the lobby. They expelled a stream of residents. Nobody acknowledged the woman. Several elevators opened and closed before we could reach one. We stepped inside and the woman pushed the button for the eleventh floor. She became quiet, perhaps lost in thought. We were alone and I felt anxious.

During the ride up, I hoped the woman's apartment was close to the elevator.

It wasn't.

We trudged down a long hall. When we reached her door, I extended the grocery bag toward her.

"Here you go," I said.

She didn't take the bag. She placed the cane on her arm and fumbled in her purse for her keys. She unlocked the door and shifted aside.

"You can set that in the kitchen," she said.

I wasn't physically afraid of the woman. But I did wonder whether somebody else was waiting inside.

I warily entered the apartment. The drapes were closed and it was dark. I paused and let my eyes adjust to the light. I heard the woman shift behind me. She shut the door and flipped a light switch. I scanned the room. The furniture was plain and sparse. No pictures hung from the walls. There were no knickknacks about, nothing to give me a fix on the woman.

I was relieved to see the narrow kitchen, immediately to my left, just off the door. It wouldn't be far to go if I had to flee.

I set the groceries on the counter, next to the refrigerator. The woman leaned against the opposite counter. We were a foot apart. Everything was silent and still.

"There you go," I said, squeezing past her.

"Please put them away."

I almost said, "Excuse me?" But I knew I had heard her right.

I reached into the bag and watched in disbelief as my hand pulled out a head of broccoli, a cantaloupe, some lettuce, a few bananas, cans of soup, bacon and a pint of praline ice cream.

The woman told me to set the fruit on top of the refrigerator, which was already crowded with other produce. She had me stack the soup in the cupboard, which already swelled with cans. I put the ice cream in the freezer, where several other pints already gathered frost.

I opened the refrigerator. The shelves and compartments were packed. The woman told me where to set the lettuce, broccoli and bacon. I didn't think it would all fit and told her so. She insisted there was room. I wedged the items inside and closed the door before anything could fall out.

"Well, I better get going," I said.

"Hold on," the woman said.

She reached into her purse.

I wondered how much she'd try to pay me. A dollar? A quarter? I rehearsed my refusal in my head: No, that's okay. It was my pleasure. Really.

The woman withdrew her hand from her purse. She held something, but it wasn't money.

They were the biggest pair of earrings I'd ever seen. Monstrous, outrageous, lobe-stretching ornaments. And they were shaped like Africa. The entire continent. Glass chips of different colors defined Africa's several dozen countries. It was all to scale, so a single green chip represented Djibouti while the Sudan was indicated by a gob of magenta chips.

The woman extended the earrings to me.

"Help me put these on," she said.

I was amused but mostly mortified. I'd never done that—put earrings on somebody's ears. This was not for me.

I recalled the woman's motto. She had to do things herself or she wouldn't win. I reminded her of that.

Ever since her stroke, she said, she couldn't put on her own earrings. It was one of the few tasks she needed help with. She hadn't been able to wear earrings in ages; nobody was ever around to assist. She wanted to go to the La Valencia, a fancy hotel overlooking the Pacific Ocean. She wanted to look her best. She wanted to wear earrings.

"I don't think I can do it," I said.

"Sure you can," she said.

"What's at the La Valencia?"

She let loose with a throaty, lustful laugh.

"Men!" she said.

I studied her crooked smile and her pleading eyes. I held out my hand.

The earrings had to be clip-ons, I figured. Nothing that gargantuan could possibly hang from tiny holes in the skin. But I glimpsed the stems and knew the earrings were meant for pierced ears. The procedure would require an added level of intimacy.

"I really can't do this," I said.

"You can do it."

I held up the earrings. They looked like license plates dangling from deep-sea fishing hooks.

The woman leaned over the counter and cocked her head, presenting her left ear. The lobe was wrinkled, with flakes of dead skin. I could barely make out the piercing. The hole had nearly fused back together.

I aimed the earring stem at the tiny speck of a hole. The earring was so big it blocked my view. I kept tilting the earring to try and see behind it. The stem finally settled on the rim of the piercing. I pushed downward on the stem, gently. It would not go through. I pushed harder but it still wouldn't budge. I grew queasy when I concluded I couldn't get the earring in without actually touching the woman's ear.

I slipped the tip of my index finger behind the woman's earlobe to offer some resistance. I pushed again on the stem and felt it advance, but it stopped short of poking out the other side. The back of the woman's earlobe bulged from the pressure.

"I don't think it's gonna go," I said.

"It'll go."

I pushed harder. The stem wouldn't advance.

"Go ahead," the woman said.

"I don't want to hurt you."

"You're not gonna hurt me."

"I'm afraid I'm going to tear your ear."

"You're not going to tear my ear."

I tugged on her earlobe and the hole widened a bit. I wiggled the stem and bore down.

"It's not gonna go," I said, grunting.

"It'll go! It'll go!"

I was suddenly hot. My hands and underarms were sweating. I was now pressed against the woman. I couldn't believe what I was doing. I laughed; only I wasn't positive it was laughter. I wanted to drop the earring and run.

"Go ahead!" the woman yelled. "It'll go!"

I stretched her earlobe out farther and drove down harder. Whatever was holding up the stem finally let go and the metal poked through the other side.

"See? I told you!" the woman said. "That didn't hurt a bit."

I exhaled and secured the earring with a rubber safety back. I was halfway home.

The woman turned around. I didn't waste any time with her right ear. I wasn't at all delicate. I stretched her earlobe straight out from her head and manipulated it between my thumb and index finger. The piercing hole felt like a seed embedded in her skin. I jabbed the stem into the hole and squeezed down hard with both hands. My stomach fluttered when the stem jutted out the back.

"There you go!" the woman said.

Later, after she had changed her clothes and done her makeup, I drove the woman to the La Valencia. She tilted way back in that busted seat, ready for liftoff. The pendulous earrings rested on her shoulders. I could make out Algeria on top and South Africa on the bottom. And over in the upper right was Egypt. It was easy to spot because of the string of blue glass chips that signified the Nile, the longest river in the world. The thing about a river is that you will always know where you're going, but you can never foresee the twists and turns along the way.

ENCOUNTERS

"Every hundred feet the world changes."
—Roberto Bolaño

THE GRINGO'S SHOES

I kept company a while in Central America with a pretty Peace Corps volunteer from Mississippi who grabbed me on a rooftop one night and kissed me. It had been fun, and now it wasn't.

We were holed up in a one-room hovel in Santa Bárbara, Honduras, with four of her Peace Corps buddies, all women. It was pouring rain. The woman of the house was the local volunteer. She told me to leave my shoes outside even though her place was already a mess. All five women smoked and joked and drank the local firewater until the wee hours. I had no idea what I was doing there. I looked forward to hopping a bus the next day and whatever came next. I could've made an effort, but I curled up on the cement floor in a corner of the room and silently damned the cigarettes and cackling. I was determined to have a thoroughly miserable time, a goal I reached the next morning, when I discovered my shoes were missing from the porch.

A barbed-wire fence surrounded the tiny house, but the thought that someone might steal my shoes never occurred to me. They were a pair of white Nike Air Jordan cross-trainers I'd picked up during a recent visit to the States. I think I'd paid one hundred dollars for them, which felt like a large sum at the time. They were my only shoes, and I doubted I could find another pair in size twelve of any brand anywhere in that small town.

A ten-year-old girl who ran errands for the local Peace Corps volunteer offered to help look for my shoes. She was a skinny, happy child with a deep, raspy voice, and when she smiled, her nose crinkled and one eye closed.

The home where my shoes went missing stood on a steep dirt road, which had turned to mud with the overnight rain. I started the search dressed in socks but discarded them when they stuck in the mire.

The girl led me by the hand to the top of the road. A boy who lived up there was out late last night and may have seen something, she said. Along the way, she proudly pointed out her school, an unadorned cinderblock room with no glass in the windows.

The boy wasn't home. His mother, who held an infant to her chest, thought we were accusing her son of stealing my shoes. We assured her that wasn't the case, and she promised to question her son the moment he returned.

No robbers lived in this barrio, the girl told me with authority; whoever took the shoes lived somewhere else. But she figured somebody knew something. She knocked on the door of every house all the way down the hill. The homes were bare shacks, with no electricity or running water, and most had dirt floors. It was a poor neighborhood but a proud one. Everyone expressed great concern that the gringo's shoes had been taken in their part of town. Some looked downright embarrassed. Several joined in the search.

Soon, a crowd had gathered in the muddy street. Everybody knew about my shoes—not of their disappearance, but of their existence.

"We saw them sitting out there at eleven last night," a woman said.

"I saw them, too," a man chimed in.

"Yes, yes," a boy said excitedly. "Nikes."

The arrival of my Nikes in Santa Bárbara was like the circus coming to town. While I slept, locals had assembled at the barbed-wire fence to gawk at the gringo's one-hundred-dollar pair of sneakers.

An old woman cursed the thieves. The town had a gang of bad boys, she said, it was true. Her grandson sometimes associated with the gang. She did not approve, but she was certain her grandson didn't take the shoes. She cursed the thieves again.

The woman from the top of the hill, still carrying the baby, arrived with her son in tow. He swore he didn't see who took my shoes, and I believed him.

More residents left their shanties and joined us in the road. There were more vows to help me find my Nikes. The search party now numbered twenty or so, and I grew overwhelmed by the attention.

Travel is a great teacher. Even when you're lazy and not even looking to learn anything new, lessons just keep coming at you.

I looked around the crowd. Some people hung their heads in shame. I followed their downcast eyes and, now seeing what I had missed all along, also felt ashamed. A few of the folks helping find the gringo's shoes wore cheap plastic shower sandals. The rest of them, like me, stood barefoot in the mud.

The night before, I wondered why on earth I had come here. Now I knew.

ONE DAY

It was an early morning at my cabin in Antigua, on the mountainside across from the Río Pensativo. I awoke with Andrea beside me in bed. She was not yet my wife, but I knew that she would be.

This was Andrea's second trip down to Guatemala in the previous three months. We'd met on my birthday five years earlier. We'd had our moments, but we'd also been the victims of bad timing. Either she had a boyfriend or I had a girlfriend. Now both of us were unattached. We lived in different countries, but that wasn't a huge obstacle. It was our time.

Andrea had to fly home to San Diego on that evening's red-eye. We didn't figure to get out of bed for breakfast, and maybe not even for lunch.

Then the Irishman turned up, bellowing his brogue.

I flung open one of the colored-glass sliding doors that formed the front of the cabin. The Irishman looked like he hadn't gone to bed since we'd closed down Latino's bar a few hours earlier. An ex-rugby player, he was a big man who blocked my view of the volcanoes in the background.

I peered around him and saw Andrea's rental car. She had let the Irishman drive himself home the previous night. Now he had driven the car clear up the mountainside, even though there was no road.

The Irishman loved to drive. But he'd been roaming around Latin America for years by bus and hadn't had the chance. He asked us to go for a long drive.

Andrea and I smiled at each other. What was one day? We had a lifetime ahead of us.

The three of us headed north through the highlands, the Irishman behind the wheel. He was an aggressive driver, revving it to ninety on the occasional straightaway, and zipping through every turn. The steering wheel was on the other side of the car from those in Ireland—and he had to drive on the right rather than the left—but this didn't slow him down.

Past Salamá, we pulled into the Biotopo del Quetzal, a reserve for Guatemala's national bird. We scrambled over the fern-draped mountains, searching for the elusive quetzal, but we were unable to spot one. It didn't matter. The waterfalls from the cascading Río Colorado were lovely, and, for once, I felt completely at ease.

Deep in the forest, Andrea and I posed for a photo. When she mailed me a duplicate the following week, I studied it carefully. It was slightly blurry—the Irishman's hand must have jiggled when he snapped the picture. But you could still see we were happy and in love. When I looked at that photo, I saw my future—and I liked what I saw.

I'd already given notice to my landlord. The only thing keeping me in Antigua was a travel article I'd promised a magazine. I needed about a month, and I could make

California by New Year's. Then Andrea and I would have our fresh start.

Before Andrea's flight from Guatemala City, we stopped for dinner at an upscale restaurant in the Zona Viva. The three of us ordered juicy steaks, and the waiter prepared our Caesar salads tableside. We splurged on beers imported from Mexico rather than drinking the local Gallo, which always had a funky taste to it. I was content and lucky. (The next night two tourists were robbed and gunned down leaving the same restaurant. I felt terrible for the victims, and I was grateful Andrea's flight wasn't a day later.)

At the airport, I accompanied Andrea to check-in and then walked her to the immigration line. We held each other, neither of us wanting to let go.

"Come home, Mike," she said.

"I will," I said.

And I did, but not for another three years.

NEEDS

I needed a home and a desk. Some folks said I needed more.

This was in Huehuetenango, in the highlands of western Guatemala. I stopped there because I liked the sound of the name—way-way-ten-ANG-o. But I mainly stopped because I was too knackered to travel any farther.

My on-again, off-again engagement to Anne was off again. This time for good. I left San Francisco with little more than my clothes. Didn't even take my bowling ball, the one I bought for a quarter at a yard sale when Anne and I were furnishing our apartment. The holes of the bowling ball fit my fingers and, coincidentally, it was already monogrammed, "Mike." I had taken this as a sign, but now it felt like bad luck.

I drifted south to a friend's in San Diego. Once I had a plan I traveled overland through Mexico for the next seventy-two hours. When I crossed into Guatemala, a chicken bus delivered me to the outskirts of Huehuetenango. I couldn't bear another bus ride. After three days and nights of sitting upright, my legs were numb and a lump the size of a walnut had formed below my right buttock. So I limped the last few kilometers into town.

I liked Huehuetenango immediately. The locals were pleasant, and so was their central park, and there were few tourists. The place was loaded with Mormon missionaries, but I knew we'd be running in different circles.

One of the other gringos I saw was a British diabetic, who was laid low with a bad stomach bug. We were both guests at the same budget inn a few blocks from the plaza. I'd bring him chicken broth a couple times a day and make sure he remembered his insulin injections.

Then there was the chain-smoking Eskimo who stayed in the room next to mine. He wore a hooded parka despite the eighty-degree weather. He usually had it zipped down, and since he didn't bother with a shirt his big brown belly was exposed. He kept two packs of smokes in one jacket pocket and two lighters in the other. He spoke to me only once. While I sipped coffee on the patio one morning, he popped his head out of his room and declared, "God is not alive," then closed the door.

When the Eskimo checked out, three Guatemalan women moved into his old room. I heard them before dawn, complaining to the world that there was no hot water. The inn had a resident parrot named Lola, and for the rest of the day it screeched, *"No hay agua caliente!"*

The three women were sisters from Guatemala City, the capital. They were searching for their father. The country was still embroiled in a civil war and thousands of citizens had gone missing. The sisters suspected their father was dead. Still, they had to make an effort.

The oldest sister told me their bus was robbed the previous day and they lost all their money. She had managed to hide her necklace from the bandits. She sold it to continue the search for her father, but the local jeweler didn't give her much for it.

She said that since she had shared her problems with me, I must now share mine with her. I told her I didn't have any problems.

"Everybody has problems," she said in Spanish.

"Maybe," I said, "but mine are tiny compared to yours."

"Tell me."

So I told her about Anne and the bowling ball.

"Was your fiancée pretty?" she said.

"Very."

"That was your mistake."

I looked at her.

"Never marry a pretty woman," she said. "Pretty women are careless. Marry an ugly woman instead. Ugly women are sincere."

As I pondered that, she offered to become my wife.

"Pero tú eres muy bonita," I said.

She scoffed at me and rejoined her sisters.

During the days, I wrote in my room, and in the late afternoons I took long walks along a dirt road leading away from town. The road wended past the shops of artisans, and several of the artisans' kids would tag along with me. A few dogs usually joined us.

In the evenings, after a dinner of rice and beans, I'd generally call around at the corner *mercado* to practice my Spanish with the locals. The grocer was excited to learn I was from the U.S. He had a daughter who lived there.

"Where?" I said.

"Louisiana," he said. "No, Louisville."

The grocer wasn't sure which and asked if I had a map. I didn't, but I drew him one on a piece of butcher paper. A crowd gathered to watch as I sketched the Southeastern U.S. and penciled in the names of some of the cities.

"Louisiana," the grocer said, tapping the pencil on the boot-shaped state. "*Sí, Sí,* Baton Rouge."

He fished his Guatemalan passport from his pocket. He planned to visit his daughter soon and had recently obtained a U.S. visa. The locals took turns inspecting the visa, tilting it under the light to view the hologram of the American bald eagle embedded in the grocer's photograph. The grocer beamed with pride.

The woman who owned the inn had a brother, a dentist, who was building an addition to his house and wanted to rent it out. The dentist drove me to take a look. The new wing would have its own bedroom, bath and kitchen, and it fronted a shady courtyard. The dentist said it would be ready in ten days. But ten days became twenty, then thirty, and I never moved in.

A couple other leads proved equally fruitless. The restaurant with overhead quarters for rent played loud music all night and was infested with rats. And when I answered a bulletin board notice for an apartment for rent, I found a single windowless room that shared a bathroom with seven other residents, including two missionaries.

Somebody suggested I go see the owner of the local radio station. He had a place for rent.

The radio station owner was an energetic, jolly fellow. He invited me into his office and poured me some coffee.

"I hear you have an apartment for rent," I said.

"An apartment, no," he said. "I have a house, a new house. It is beautiful. You must see it. It has four bedrooms and a garage."

"Oh," I said. "I don't have a car, and it's only me, so I don't need four bedrooms."

"No problem, I have an idea."

He stepped around his desk and swept his arm across the spacious office, where four women pecked away on typewriters.

"None of my secretaries is married," he said, loud enough for everyone to hear. "You should all move in together."

I was flustered and said the only thing I could think of.

"Why aren't these pretty ladies married?" I asked the boss.

"Because each of them is waiting for an American, six-foot-four, with blond hair and blue eyes," he said, describing me.

All of the secretaries laughed, and a couple of them looked up from their typewriters at me.

The boss addressed one of his secretaries, a handsome woman with short brown hair, glasses and gleaming white teeth.

"You should move in with him," he told her.

She blushed and giggled, then rallied with a crack about how our widely divergent heights might pose a challenge in bed.

I allowed the image to linger a while before I politely agreed and left.

My room at the inn had no desk or chair, and I had to write while reclining on the bed. Other than that I was content there. The owner knocked the rate down from five dollars per night to four, including a daily breakfast of cornflakes, hot milk and a banana.

The least expensive desk at the local furniture store sold for seventy-five *quetzales*, roughly thirteen dollars. I told the woman who ran the business I didn't want to spend that much because I'd be leaving Huehuetenango within a few months. In that case, the woman said, she'd loan me the desk.

I had recently completed a journey across America with no money, not a single penny, and I was writing a book about the experience. So many people had helped me along the way. Even those with little to spare had given freely of their food and shelter. It had been overwhelming—and I was tired of taking.

I told the woman in the furniture store I'd prefer to rent her desk.

She insisted I borrow it.

I said I'd feel a whole lot better if she'd let me pay her something.

She reluctantly agreed.

"How much?" I said.

She thought a moment and replied, "Five quetzales."

"Five quetzales," I repeated. "For how long?"

"For as long as you need it," she said, and smiled.

I carried the desk back to my room and set it near the edge of the bed, in front of a window that looked out on the green mountains in the distance. It was a simple, unfinished desk with no drawers. But seeing it in my room made me happy. The top of the desk was flat and its four legs reached the floor. Someday I'd find a house, and maybe even a wife, but on that afternoon in Huehuetenango, I had everything I needed.

SEXY BEAST

When we moved there, New York felt like an extended holiday. Andrea had a temporary job assignment with her company. I had a new book contract. We'd be returning to California within two years, so there was no pressure. Finally, the city that had always seen me at my lowest was now uplifting and magnetic.

One of the appealing things about New York this time was our new home. We lived on MacDougal Street, in Greenwich Village. We rented the ground-floor apartment of a four-story neocolonial building, one of twenty-two houses in the MacDougal-Sullivan Gardens Historic District. These houses line one side each of MacDougal and Sullivan Streets, between Bleecker and Houston Streets. The resulting one-block rectangle surrounds an urban greenbelt. Each house has its own backyard. Beyond these stands a common garden, with a lawn, mature trees, shrubs, hedges, flagstone paths and a small basketball court. Once a year residents meet in the middle for Digging Day, when they plant new flowers and have a picnic. From the frenetic sidewalk, there's no evidence of the serene swath hidden inside. It's a unique space and we were lucky to live there.

Anna Wintour, editor of *Vogue*, lived across the garden from us. Richard Gere was a few doors down from her. The painter Francesco Clemente and his family lived on our side of the garden, in a doublewide townhouse formerly occupied by Bob Dylan.

Many of the other homeowners had grown up in their houses, including our landlady. She now lived on the top floor with her husband, an older fellow with a wooden leg who had worked all over the world. He was a real character. When residents complained about noise from a nearby nightclub, he convened a meeting to discuss the issue. The name of the nightclub was Life.

"Life," he said, "it's been around for millions of years, but it just got a lot more complicated."

There had been a long list of applicants for our apartment. The landlady said she picked us because she knew we'd appreciate the yard and garden. We truly did, largely because of our dog Maya. While many sleepy New Yorkers had to escort their dogs down to the street for midnight potty runs, we had the luxury of opening the French doors at the foot of our bed and letting Maya out.

The children who lived in the other houses of the historic district kept Maya entertained. These New York kids had to be jaded by celebrity, because they always bypassed our neighbor's dog, who played Sandy in the revival of the Broadway musical *Annie*, to romp with Maya in our backyard.

Maya had appeared in our San Diego neighborhood a year earlier. She had no collar or tags, and when Andrea couldn't find her owner, she took her in. She was a strikingly gorgeous hound of some undeterminable mix. Her best features were her brindle coat (or "jacket," as I called it) and fetching smile.

Maya had turned heads in San Diego, but in New York she was a superstar. She was one of those rare individuals who thrive under the bright lights and scrutiny of the big city. She had the look and she knew how to rock it. Construction workers wolf-whistled at her. Homeless men insisted she take their hard-won food. People who wanted to hug her or have their picture taken with her constantly stopped us on the street. A ten-minute stroll could easily take an hour. It got so bad we considered disguising her in a scarf and giant sunglasses, à la Jackie Onassis.

When out and about, Maya hated to walk across subway grates in the sidewalk. But the few times she couldn't avoid them she'd go with it. She'd strike a pose and allow the updraft to billow her hair, just like Marilyn Monroe in that famous photo.

Each morning, I'd sit Maya outside the Starbucks on Sixth Avenue and hope to heck she wasn't kidnapped for ransom during the minute or two it took to buy my latte. We'd then walk over to a bench in Washington Square Park, where I'd finish my coffee and read the *Times*. Afterwards, I'd unleash Maya inside the dog run, where she was always the center of attention with both humans and other hounds. I can't count the times someone ignored their dog and fawned all over Maya and asked me what kind of breed she was. The rule of the dog run was that you had to pick up after your dog. But I rarely had to do this because one of Maya's many fans would usually beat me to it, as if it were an honor.

Like any star, Maya endured her share of spite and jealousy. At the photo shoot for the annual calendar of the Washington Square Park Dog Run, Maya was positioned front and center. But when the calendar was released, she didn't get her own month, and she had been airbrushed out of the cover image.

Maya was also a threat to New York's modeling community. Whenever I walked her in SoHo, insecure models would scurry to the opposite sidewalk to avoid sharing the same catwalk, as it were. When we passed by the picture window of Raoul's, the toothpick-thin waifs huddled at the bar inside would stare into their soda waters and throw Maya the cold, bony shoulder. It was savagely petty, but Maya remained oblivious to the slight.

I often joked that our renowned neighbor Clemente—whose art has been exhibited at the Guggenheim, the Royal Academy and the Uffizi—might like to paint Maya. (At least I think it was a joke.) That never happened, but I did find a death row inmate who painted animal portraits for seventy-five dollars, ninety dollars framed. When I mailed Maya's photo to the Texas prison, I wrote the inmate that the reason Andrea and I named our dog Maya was because we loved the Mayan culture of southern Mexico and northern Central America. The inmate mailed me back a perfect rendering of Maya, posing under a blood orange sky at the base of a Mayan temple. Maya left this world many years ago (I don't know the fate of the death row inmate), but that kitschy painting still hangs in my office and never fails to amuse me.

It was also in New York that Maya was given the nickname that would stick for the rest of her life. She had a thing for crosswalks. Her gait changed and she took her time passing before the stopped traffic. I think she viewed a crosswalk as her own private fashion runway. I swear you could see her sashay and shimmy. One time, she lingered too long in the crosswalk and the light changed. A horn sounded. It wasn't an irate motorist. It was just another of Maya's many admirers—a smitten cabbie.

The cabbie leaned out of the taxi window.

"You sexy beast!" he hollered, then bit down hard on his hand.

A GOOD LIFE

At Unawatuna, on the south coast of Sri Lanka, humongous Russian tourists sat at plastic tables in the sand, smoking cigarettes while hunched over their laptops. They were slathered in sun oil, and when they waddled the few steps to the sea, they practically spilled out of their Speedos and bikinis. One man, gut jiggling, lumbered down the beach after a sand crab, trying to film it with his iPhone.

The pimply-faced bartender looked on impassively. I ordered a Lion Lager from him and commented on how close the outdoor café was to the Indian Ocean. The café was of the same recent vintage as the other restaurants and hotels up and down the crescent-shaped beach, their predecessors wiped out by the 2004 tsunami. After the tragedy claimed the lives of 35,000 Sri Lankans, the government banned construction within one hundred meters of the high tide line—but the law was widely ignored. Every so often, the bartender said, waves washed over the legs of the stool I sat on.

The bartender was twelve years old when the tsunami struck. His family's home was five meters from the ocean.

"How did you survive?" I asked.

"I am Buddhist," the bartender said. "I did good in last life, so I live in this life."

In the moments before the wall of water landed on their house, the bartender's father futilely barricaded the front door with furniture. The wave crashed in, and the bartender and his little brother and their father clung to the swirling tables and chairs as they swiftly rose to the ceiling. The father was knocked unconscious and sank, and the little brother was trapped in a whirlpool. The bartender dived below to find a way out.

"I can go deep," he said.

He located a window, but it was shuttered. He frantically kicked at it until it broke open. He returned for his brother and father and pulled them to the surface.

"We came up, nobody is swimming—nobody to help," he said. "The people who do good in last life live, and the people who do bad die."

"You're a hero," I said, "so you will do well in the next life, too."

"Yes," he said with a little laugh.

The bartender told me that in the days following the tsunami, the rumor was the United States had caused it.

"Many people say your people make bomb in water," he said.

"Really?"

"Yes."

"Did you believe that?"

"No," he said. "But some people still believe that."

I took a swig of beer and glanced at the corpulent Russians splashing in the sea. To some islanders who recalled the Cold

War, when the U.S. tested nukes in the Pacific, the rumor probably made sense.

"You think the world will end?" the bartender asked me.

I was momentarily befuddled, then remembered we were nearing the end of the year 2012. Many believed that an ancient Mayan calendar predicted mankind would cease to exist on December 21, 2012.

"The Mayan calendar?" I asked the bartender.

"Yes."

"They had a different calendar, it doesn't match the modern one," I said. "What about you? Do you think the world will end this year?"

"No," the bartender said.

But he was a Buddhist who had lived a good life. He knew he was set. Me? What the hell did I know? And so I waited until 2013 to write this.

THE AMAZING DR. X

Soon after I arrived in Juticalpa, Honduras, I kept hearing about a certain Dr. X: brilliant physician, humanitarian, impractical joker, alcoholic, lunatic. Everyone I met had a story about him.

Juticalpa is the capital of the department of Olancho, dubbed "the Wild East" for its outlaw ways, and Dr. X fit right in. He creeped you out with his huge bug eyes, bulging even more behind his Coke-bottle glasses. Mental illness ran in his family. When he brought friends home as a child, his mother dropped to the floor and flopped around like a fish. "Come on, everybody," she'd say, "let's go swimming!" This didn't prevent him from achieving the highest scores in his nation's history on his medical board exams, or from learning seven languages, including Greek and Japanese. He also had a photographic memory.

Dr. X instructed his patients to arrive at his office at four in the morning so he could end each workday by eight a.m. and go drinking. His closest friends were fellow drunks, and he supplied them with bottles of one hundred percent alcohol. He once took a drinking buddy to an international medical conference in Costa Rica. He dressed the drunk up in a suit and tie and introduced him as an esteemed surgeon from

Honduras. The drunk delivered a paper, prepared by Dr. X, and received a standing ovation.

Dr. X's methods were unorthodox, but effective. He once decided to rid a village of appendicitis, so he removed the appendix of every peasant. During office hours, he divided his patients into three groups—"diarrhea," "colds" and "other"—then gave them all the same prescription. He advised his poor *campesino* patients to watch their diets: "Don't eat caviar," he told them. "Stay away from white truffles. And avoid Kobe beef." When performing surgery, he'd often bathe himself in blood, march into the waiting room, stare gravely at the patient's family while panting, then march back into the operating room.

Dr. X had a small ranch where he named his livestock after medicines—Amoxicillin, Ibuprofen, Lidocaine, and so on. He was a poor provider to his twenty-six children (by several different women), mainly because his patients rarely paid him, though a few bartered animals for his services. Dr. X once got a loan for a car but started missing payments after three months. The bank wrote him letters demanding its money. Dr. X sent the bank an iguana that had been given to him for services rendered. He attached a note to the iguana stating the reptile had the potential to lay twelve eggs and thus was the equivalent of three car payments.

After he was elected mayor of Juticalpa, Dr. X reached out to world leaders for aid to his impoverished town. Sadly, assistance was rarely forthcoming. He once wrote former Nicaraguan dictator Anastasio Somoza, asking him for money to help rid Olancho of communists. Somoza didn't comply, but he did write back, "I like your plan." (Dr. X framed the letter and hung it on his office wall.) Dr. X also wrote the Pope, who refused his request to send the women of Juticalpa one million birth control pills. But when Dr. X attended an international mayors' conference in Tokyo, he managed to land a meeting with some prominent members of the Japanese government. They listened attentively as Dr. X delivered his impassioned plea for a badly needed hospital in Juticalpa. The Japanese officials were so taken by the strange, bug-eyed Honduran who spoke their language that they agreed to build the hospital.

I stayed in Juticalpa for a week. I met several people who offered to introduce me to the amazing Dr. X, including some of his drinking buddies. For whatever reason, our paths never crossed. On my way out of town, however, I passed by Juticalpa's lone hospital. It looked busy. It stood there gleaming in the hot sun, a monument to just how far a whole lot of crazy can carry you in this world.

MARRIAGE AND CHINESE FOOD

In Jodhpur, India, after touring the Mehrangarh Fort, we ate at a modest Chinese restaurant on the edge of the city. I shouldn't have been surprised the food was good because I don't recall ever having a bad Chinese meal anywhere in the world. Whether in Ecuador, Hungary, South Africa or India, it's always struck me as the cuisine that travels best.

Toward the end of dinner, the chef appeared at our table to ask how everything was.

"Delicious!" I said.

The chef's name was Leslie and he was thirty-four. He was born in Kolkata to an Indian woman who couldn't afford to keep him. When he was one week old, a couple from Kolkata's large Chinese community adopted him. They ran a Chinese restaurant and he grew up in the kitchen. He later worked as a chef for a five-star hotel and the catering division of Air India. Now he was making a go of his own restaurant in Rajasthan.

The chef had a pronounced snaggletooth, which he tried to cover by stretching his lips. It was a losing battle, however, as he was always smiling.

"Are you married?" I asked.

"Of course!" he said.

He told me his wife was originally from Bangladesh, and they had met in Kolkata.

I looked around the restaurant, wondering where she might be.

The chef, anticipating my next question, said, "She's in Kolkata."

"Visiting?"

"No, living."

Once a year, the chef traveled eleven hundred miles east to Kolkata to see his wife. After a few days, he returned to Jodhpur, and they wouldn't meet again until the next year.

"Wow, you must miss her a lot," I said.

"Not so much," the chef said, then laughed. "Too close, a little sour. Far away, sweet. Sweet and sour—like the food."

THE VILLA DELFINA

I've lived in thirty-nine homes. That I can recall, anyway. By homes, I mean residences where I received mail, whether it was birthday cards as a kid or absentee ballots once I became of age. My favorite of those thirty-nine homes was the Villa Delfina.

Both "Villa" and "Delfina" were misnomers. The place was a one-bedroom cottage with a tin roof. And I never once saw a dolphin in Antigua, that gorgeous colonial city set in the central highlands of Guatemala. Yet dangling from a bamboo lamppost beneath an expansive pine tree outside the front door was a sign marked VILLA DELFINA. I'd ultimately hang a busted flip-flop from the sign. It made about as much sense as the name.

My previous dwelling was a house in La Jolla, California, which I shared with several other journalists. Fine fellows all of them, and they remain among my closest friends, but I knew our living situation was temporary, and I treated it as such. In the four years I resided at the Cherry House, as it was dubbed, a half dozen boxes of books and clothes and keepsakes remained stacked against my bedroom wall. When I arrived at the Villa Delfina, however, I unpacked completely. Of course, by then all of my possessions fit in a single duffel bag, but that little cottage was also the first place in my adult life that truly felt like home.

I had spent the previous spring in Antigua and adored it. I should never have left, but I did, and after a string of bad beats at the card tables in Vegas, I hurried back down there to regroup. When asked what I was doing, I replied, "not working," or "wearing shorts every day for a year." Truth was I didn't know. I had some notion of sitting still for a spell, ideally under a roof of my own. "Your independence is awesome," an old girlfriend had recently remarked, "but so is your lonesomeness." Then a letter from another woman I had disappointed arrived in care of general delivery. "You are disgusting, rotten, cowardly, degrading, sad, discourteous, half-assed, immature and pathetic." When I saw she had waited a year to post the letter, lonesomeness sounded attractive.

I studied the bulletin board at Doña Luisa's restaurant for rental housing. A frustrating search led only to individual rooms in private homes or to rental houses beyond my means. I answered one last ad, for a studio apartment. When I learned it was part of a busy posada, the innkeeper conceded it wouldn't give me the solitude I craved. But the man knew of a cottage that had recently been vacated, and he offered to take me there.

We walked to the outskirts of town, arriving at a massive wooden gate with a door to the side. The innkeeper rapped on the door and a shy, teenaged girl appeared. She said the owner was expected back later that afternoon. The innkeeper asked if we could take a peek at the cottage, and the girl let us in.

Once inside, I saw that the wooden gate hid a sprawling compound. The girl and her family lived in the large, airy house at the base of the property. The innkeeper and I followed a twisting lane up the hill. We came upon several prefabricated, mostly metal, cottages. They reminded me of Quonset huts, and all of them were connected. I couldn't hide my disappointment. But the innkeeper assured me the vacant cottage was further up the hill.

The lane ended and we climbed a well-tended path bordered by bougainvillea and other flowering plants. The hill grew steeper and I became aware of the many birds darting and singing in the trees. Out of breath, we stepped into a clearing. Above us, framed by palms and pines, stood the Villa Delfina. Before we had even reached the brick walkway, I was already thinking of the little cottage as mine.

I thanked the innkeeper, who returned to his posada. I was so anxious to acquire the rental that I was reluctant to leave, for fear someone else might swoop in ahead of me. I decided to await the owner's return on the street, outside the gate. When he appeared a few hours later, he turned out to be an affable, white-haired businessman from Guatemala City. The property had been in his family for generations, he said. He and his wife visited maybe once a month, staying in one of the prefab units. Apart from the family who occupied the house at the bottom of the hill, nobody else lived on the property. The place was as peaceful as it appeared. He also confirmed the cottage was vacant and for rent.

I accompanied the owner back up the hill. Moments after entering the Villa Delfina, I had agreed to rent it for seven hundred *quetzales* per month (at that time roughly one hundred thirty-five dollars). I offered the owner three months' rent in advance. He smiled at my exuberance and said that wasn't necessary. He handed me the keys and I rushed back to town to collect my things from the *hostal* where I'd been staying.

My new home was rectangular in shape, with a cement foundation and lacquered pine walls. The bedroom had a firm double bed. The living area held a faded matching loveseat and wingback chair, a round dining table and four chairs, and a cupboard that served as my dresser. An old TV that got one channel topped the cupboard. Whenever I turned it on it was airing either the movie *Goodfellas* or a children's television show hosted by the Brazilian actress-singer Xuxa.

A backdoor opened to a covered outdoor hallway that led to the bathroom. In the middle of the night, when I got up to use the toilet, I took care not to step on the spiders crawling across the tiles. A third door, at the side of the house, accessed a patio. Beyond there, a separate room contained a countertop gas stove and a deep double sink. The kitchen had no refrigerator. A tidy lawn of thick-bladed grass fronted the cottage. Croquet was an option, had there been equipment and if one didn't mind severe side-hill lies.

The Villa Delfina's best feature was its front wall, which had six wood-framed sliding glass doors. Each sliding door and its corresponding stationary panel contained four panes of opaque glass, colored orange, blue, green and purple, respectively. Whenever I slid open those doors, I gazed down on Antigua's glorious colonial buildings, including the blinding white dome of the Iglesia de San Francisco. And towering in the background, the magnificent volcanoes Agua, Fuego and Acatenango. It was a view that never failed to stir the soul.

My mornings usually started with a glass of fresh juice, squeezed from oranges plucked from trees outside the cottage. The compound was a working plot of land, with orange groves and other crops terraced higher up the hillside. A crew of six men tended the crops, cleared brush and fixed things around the property. The owner's right-hand man, Roberto, a lean fellow of about seventy who favored untucked long-sleeve dress shirts, supervised them.

Some years earlier Roberto had lived in Miami and New York City. He practiced his English on me, and I practiced my Spanish on him. Whenever he delivered my mail, which would become a daily ritual, he'd announce himself from far down the hill so as not to startle me.

"I am coming! I am coming!" he'd holler. "I am speaking English! I am speaking English!" I'd greet him at the door and he'd continue: "I am very happy and I am dancing because I believe in God and I believe in Jesus Christ." Sometimes he'd throw in a mention of the Virgin Mary. After handing me my letters, he'd dance a jig and point to the sky. Roberto may be the happiest man I've ever known.

I can't say whether I've ever been truly happy, but during my stay at the Villa Delfina I was genuinely content. I enjoyed a sense of belonging. It was one of those rare times in my life when there was absolutely nowhere else I wanted to be.

In addition to local acquaintances who'd drop by to listen to music, play dominoes or borrow my shower, I had some out-of-town visitors. My future wife, Andrea, came to see me not once, but twice. And my longtime friends Bruce and Diane flew down from the Bay Area. The Villa Delfina was also where I was living when I met my former fiancée, Anne. She was just out of college and in Antigua to study Spanish. When she returned to California, I wrote her weekly and implored her to come back. When she did, she moved into my cottage. We soon decided to marry and started making wedding plans.

I never intended to stay at the Villa Delfina as long as I did. I figured I had enough money to last four months, tops. But each time I was about to go broke, I'd land a freelance travel story, or a tax refund check would arrive, or I'd win a few quetzales off the tourists who played in a poker game I ran in a local restaurant. Before I knew it, I'd lived in that cottage for nearly a year.

A part of me wished to remain at the Villa Delfina indefinitely. I was finally pulled away by a new job and a wedding (neither of which would come to pass). However excited I was about the future, I sensed on some level that life might never be as simple and satisfying as it had been on that hillside above Antigua.

On the day I began my journey back north, I left the keys to the Villa Delfina inside on the table. I faced the door as I pulled it shut for the last time. The latch caught with a loud click. I pushed hard on the door three or four times. It was closed.

Two years later I found myself back in Antigua. One afternoon after a solid day of writing, I went for a walk to clear my head. I instinctively followed the cobbled streets to the edge of town and wandered toward that big wooden gate. I didn't have the nerve to knock and see who might answer. Roberto? The landlord? A member of the family who lived in the main house? Someone new? I glanced at the gate out of the corner of my eye and kept walking.

A few nights later, while dining out, I fell into conversation with a Canadian expatriate one stool over. He managed a boutique hotel that had opened after I left. I said I used to live in Antigua. He asked where, and when I told him he grew animated. He had been living in the Villa Delfina for two years. When he learned my name he became more excited. He had read a travel magazine piece I'd written on Antigua. What's more, he'd snapped up numerous copies of the magazine, and my article and the accompanying photos now served as wallpaper inside the cottage.

"You've got to come see the place," he said. "I've really fixed it up."

"Sure," I said.

"My next day off is Monday," he said. "How about then?"

"Sounds great."

But it was a lie. I knew I wouldn't set foot inside the Villa Delfina again. By then I had learned some closed doors are never meant to be reopened.

TRANSITIONS

Hungary was in transition, and so were Anne and I.

The Soviet Army had left. Communism was kaput. A McDonald's restaurant now anchored Budapest's Keleti train station.

Everybody in Budapest bought a dog, or two, or three. Owning a dog was a symbol of success in the new market economy. People took them everywhere: stores, restaurants, the Metro. Nobody picked up after them. Rather than walking down the sidewalks, we took our chances in the middle of the street. When the winter snows came, apartment dwellers too lazy to walk their dogs—or too poor to feed them—set them free. Packs of dogs roamed the city parks. Authorities rounded up and euthanized scores of them each day.

Another sign you had made it was the fur stole. Hungarian women favored the kind with the animal's head still attached. Sometimes, while riding the subway, I'd glance at the adjacent passenger and flinch at the sight of a wicked fox about to attack me.

All of the Americans we knew in Budapest were Hungarian-Americans, over to the old country to explore their family roots. Anne and I had no such connections. We were drifters.

We had drifted from Guatemala to California to Vermont to Hungary. An English-language newspaper had hired me.

I used to call Anne "Disco," because she had dated John Travolta. It wasn't true; it was just a story I liked to tell. I later called her Bun—I'm not even sure why. When she landed a job in Budapest, I called her Comptroller Bun. It was the last nickname I gave her.

We moved into a furnished apartment, in a classical building off Alkotás út, on the Buda side of the Danube. It had twelve-foot ceilings, a crystal chandelier and a grand piano. The family who lived there could no longer afford it, so they rented it to us for three hundred dollars per month and moved to the suburbs. The night they handed us the keys, the adult son played some boogie-woogie on the piano. He was good. We told him he should take the piano, but he said their new home was too small. We waited until he left before we lowered the piano lid and used it as a shelf for our boombox and cassettes.

Some people prospered under the new capitalist system. But many others now struggled to get by. People were desperate. There were myriad Ponzi schemes. One out of every one hundred Hungarians was now an Amway distributor. Naïve investors were swindled by peddlers of worthless dinosaur eggs, smuggled into the country from Mongolia.

Gypsies tried to pickpocket me daily. They would board a tram in front of me and only advance a step or two inside. When the doors closed behind me, I was cornered. The Gypsies would pretend to be lost tourists, pointing at maps and asking me directions while running their hands through my pockets. It never worked. It was real amateur-hour stuff, and I felt embarrassed for them.

Hungary had long led the world in suicide, but now the rate had soared. Experts spoke of the "contagion effect"—how suicide was getting passed around like a cold. One depressed farmer after another killed himself by tying a wire to his genitals and tossing the other end of the wire over a power line. There was a rash of copycat suicides at the train station where the poet Attila József had thrown himself before a train in 1937. Many others chugged whatever household chemicals they could get their hands on.

Everybody smoked, even the doctors and nurses on the hospital cancer wards. Many restaurants and taverns we frequented were underground and without windows. The smoke got so thick sometimes you couldn't read the menu. I walked around for six months with a nagging cough.

Budapest was dark and brooding and beautiful, and we were constantly treated to some strange spectacle or another. One night Anne and I attended a concert in a gymnasium. Three musicians appeared on stage. One of them played two flutes at the same time. The percussionist had a big brass ball dangling from a chain; he struck the ball with a hammer and swung it over his head like a lariat. The pianist leaned into the innards of the piano and plucked the strings while moaning and bellowing. He then took the percussionist's hammer and hammered on the strings. The guy tweaked the strings so badly the concert was delayed an hour while a piano tuner was summoned.

A few months after we arrived, Budapest grappled with a bear problem. The bears weren't exactly wild. They were performing bears smuggled over the Carpathian Mountains by Romanians who sold them to traveling circuses. Sometimes the smugglers couldn't find a buyer, so they'd set the bears free. As the economy worsened, most of the traveling circuses folded, and the number of bears unleashed on the city multiplied. They were both a nuisance and a danger.

Language was a real barrier. I didn't speak Hungarian and most Hungarians didn't speak English. On many stories, one of the newspaper's photographers acted as my translator. He and his wife had us over for dinner once. His wife and their five-year-old daughter didn't speak English, so the photographer translated for all of us.

At one point, the little girl buried her face in her mother's chest and softly murmured something. The photographer and his wife looked aghast.

"What did she say?" I asked.

"It was nothing," the photographer said.

When I pressed him, the photographer's wife, who must have deduced what I had asked, shook her head.

"Come on, tell us," Anne said.

The photographer finally replied, "She said, 'I don't like the guests.'"

Anne and I couldn't stop laughing.

I thought the photographer and his wife might serve us goulash, but they didn't. I ate a lot of goulash as a kid. It was one of my mom's go-to recipes. Hungarian goulash, she called it. When I moved to Budapest, I figured there'd be no way to avoid goulash. It was supposedly Hungary's national dish, after all. But I had yet to encounter it after several months. I began to think it was a myth. In the end, I never ate goulash the whole time I lived over there. I never even saw it. I never saw the bears, either.

SAD BUT TRUE

Bhutan is extraordinary. Virgin forests cover eighty-five percent of the country. The Himalayas, many topping 25,000 feet, are always in view. There isn't a single stoplight or billboard in the land. Its 700,000 citizens appear genuinely content. And relatively few tourists have yet to visit the kingdom, which only emerged from self-imposed isolation a few decades ago. The tradeoff is that independent travel is forbidden. You are attached to a guide and driver the whole way.

Andrea and I lucked out with our driver, Mr. Khandu, a cheerful, betel-chewing lookalike for Oddjob, the chauffeur/assassin from the Bond flick, *Goldfinger*. An army soldier on leave, he bore a wicked scar down one cheek, which he may or may not have sustained while fighting alongside the previous king in the campaign to rid the country of Indian terrorists.

Our guide, Ugyen (ooo-gan), was of a different cut. A sullen young man with wide-set, Marty Feldman eyes, he was nearly incomprehensible. What's worse, he was likely suffering from a broken heart, for he listened to the same sappy love song by some Bhutanese boy band again and again on the car stereo.

"I'm trying to learn the words," he announced one day.

We didn't understand any of the lyrics, but the chorus sounded like: "Sad but true/Baby, sad but true…" Thus, our catch phrase for the journey became "sad but true." As in: "Ugyen is playing 'Sad but True' for the twenty-third time today" (Andrea). "Sad but true" (me).

Bhutan is a Buddhist country, and visual reminders of this are everywhere. The place is swarming with monks. All trails and roads lead to a monastery or two (or three dozen). And you can't drive far without detouring, clockwise, around a stupa. But the most ubiquitous symbols are the ever-present strings of festive prayer flags—alternating cloth squares of blue, green, red, yellow and white—fluttering across the land. They're strung through forests, across bridges and over mountain passes. (Larger, single-colored, vertical prayer flags flap atop houses and from tall wooden poles dotting the hillsides.) Buddhists believe that the prayers inscribed on the flags are carried by the wind out to all sentient beings.

When trekking, we frequently ducked under the whimsical patches of cloth that crisscrossed every path. Bhutan was wrapped in so much material, we felt like we were traveling through an endless Christo installation.

Most days involved a hike of one to six hours to a monastery where we'd see golden statues of this guru, that lama or those consorts. Sometimes we'd hike straight uphill for hours to reach a monastery that was closed. (One locked door held a month-old bill from the power company for twenty-five *ngultrum*—about fifty cents.) It didn't matter; for us, it was more about the walks through the stunning forests, the roar of the raging rivers, and the sight of eagles soaring above.

On Descension Day, when it is believed the Buddha returned to earth, we climbed to nearly fourteen thousand feet to a monastery complex dusted with snow. We were accompanied by young, enthusiastic pilgrims who shared their tea, snacks and bubblegum with us. On other treks, we didn't encounter another person.

One day we arrived at a temple where the lone monk beckoned us to make an offering and roll the three sacred dice. I rolled a propitious number, sixteen, right out of the box. But Andrea rolled one heavy number after another. The monk, Mr. Khandu and Ugyen shook their heads and murmured gravely. Finally, Mr. Khandu waved burning incense beneath Andrea's hand, and she rolled a number that allowed the world to spin another day.

In Thimphu, the capital, Mr. Khandu stopped the car in the middle of the road, removed his Nike golf hat and quit spitting his betel juice—a mildly narcotic concoction of areca nut, betel leaf and lime (the white powder, not the fruit). The previous king rode by in a Toyota Land Cruiser. He is a revered man who abdicated the throne in 2008 and gave democracy to his people. (His son, the current king, is a figurehead. With brilliantined hair and sideburns well below his ears, he looks like a rockabilly singer.)

The previous king coined the term Gross National Happiness. Rather than Gross National Product, he declared, Bhutan's success should be measured by its quality of life. So today in the kingdom, ecology trumps business interests, and citizens enjoy free education and health care. The previous king has been called a visionary, but it's no secret how he honed his diplomatic skills—he's married to four sisters.

Bhutanese architecture bears some mention. With the exception of the chili peppers drying on the roofs and the festively painted window frames and cornices, the houses look like Swiss chalets. The other big difference being the penises, of course. Most houses in Bhutan feature hand-carved penises dangling from the four corners of the roofs. Pairs of penises are also painted near the doorways, like sentinels standing guard. These are rendered comically large (many take up entire walls) and in a state of extreme excitement. The penises aren't the doodlings of junior high school boys. Rather they are there to ward off evil demons.

Bhutan's roads offer endless thrills. They're not roads so much as horribly rutted driveways carved into sheer mountain walls, miles above valley floors. There were often road delays as workers labored to widen the "highways" from one lane to a lane and a half. As we drove farther east, ice and yaks appeared in the roads, presenting greater challenges for Mr. Khandu. The view out the window was usually a rear-end-tightening glimpse at imminent mortality. If the car did leave the road, however, there'd be ample time to text your last will and testament before hitting bottom.

In the remote Central Region, food and lodging grew more primitive. In the Phobjikha Valley, where we saw black-necked cranes migrating south from Tibet, we slept in a firetrap: ramshackle wooden structure, rooms with open-flamed stoves, and doors that locked only from the outside, à la jail cells. Our slow-witted hosts hovered uncomfortably close. It got real

Appalachian, and we feared they'd skip the banjos and head straight for the squeals.

Way out in Bumthang, we came across the finest waiter in all of Bhutan, maybe even in all of Asia. It didn't matter to him that he plied his trade in a dining room that was frigid and charmless. He'd present each dish, however bland, with impeccable efficiency and robust flair: "Potatoes, madam," he'd intone, as if they were dipped in gold…"Carrots, sir…Enjoy your cabbage." The effect was jarring, like finding a waiter from a Michelin-starred restaurant working the Kountry Korner Kafe outside Little Rock.

Toward the end of our tour, disaster struck. It was what we'd feared all along: Mr. Khandu was invaded by an evil spirit.

"It has to do with a woman," Ugyen struggled to explain.

"These things usually do," I said.

Andrea, ever more practical, inquired about our driver's symptoms, which included pains in his chest and left arm. Perhaps Mr. Khandu should immediately avail himself of Bhutan's free medical care, she suggested.

No, no, no! Ugyen insisted. A doctor might kill Mr. Khandu in his current state.

There was only one solution, Ugyen said. So he and Mr. Khandu tracked down a lama in the middle of the night. The lama performed a *puja*, a ceremony involving bowing, chanting and offerings. The lama pronounced Mr. Khandu demon free, and we were back on the road.

Knowing we had a likely cardiac case at the wheel made the return drive to Paro extra terrifying. But the puja held. Mr.

Khandu delivered us safely to the airport, and Ugyen celebrated with a back-to-back playing of "Sad but True."

DETAILS

The best travel advice I ever got came from a newsagent on the Isle of Skye. His shop overlooked Portree's pretty harbor and carried the usual newspapers and magazines, along with cigarettes, postcards, Gaelic music cassettes, scones and maps. I'd lost my road map of Scotland and popped in for a replacement.

"Doing some traveling, are ye?" the newsagent said when I asked for the Scotland road map displayed behind the counter.

"I am," I said.

"Then ye be needing this." Instead of the road map he handed me a single sheet of beige paper folded in three.

I unfolded the paper and saw what looked like a crude treasure map, with dotted lines and an X-marks-the-spot. Studying it closer, I realized it depicted a tiny portion of the west coast of Skye. There was a glorious footpath out there that shouldn't be missed, the man said. It would deliver me to a magical view of the Sea of the Hebrides. The return drive on the single-track road to the trailhead and the hike itself wouldn't take me more than a few hours out of my way.

"Sounds good," I said. I told him I'd buy the little local map, but I wanted the national map as well.

Ringing me up, the fellow locked eyes with me and said, "The details are on the ground."

I didn't know what to make of that. I hopped back in my rental car and headed away from Skye on the A87 for Fort William, Oban, Glasgow and Edinburgh. There was this long list of ruins and castles and museums I had to see. There were a lot of miles to cover. I didn't have time for any detours.

I checked off all the tourist sites and flew home. It was a perfectly fine trip—although these many years later, I recall little of what I raced around to see.

What stuck with me instead was the newsagent's comment. It took a while, but I finally got it. What I initially dismissed as a piece of Highlands gibberish became my travel mantra, and I try to keep it in mind wherever I go. When we travel, we have a choice: we can try to see it all and fail—or we can see more by looking at less. *The details are on the ground.*

A decade later, I toured Australia's island state of Tasmania. In Launceston, I entered an Irish pub where a group of local teachers hoisted pints to the memory of a colleague they'd buried that afternoon. There I met Patrick, a sixtyish high school geography teacher who wore a tweed cap and a gray beard. Whenever he made a point, he'd clap once for emphasis.

A day earlier, one of his students failed to turn in her paper on globalization. "The dog ate my computer," she said. Patrick asked if she had a backup file somewhere. The girl said she did. Patrick assumed she was bluffing, but told her to bring the paper in the next day.

"Well, she turned it in this morning, and when she did, I just put my arm around her," he said, clapping. "That moment made my year. I will always remember that moment. It makes me want to teach another six months." He beamed and sipped from his beer.

Apart from teaching, Patrick's passion was travel. He used his lengthy summer vacations to see much of the world. He was a devoted hiker, and we discovered we'd both walked several of the same trails: the Annapurna Circuit in Nepal, the Milford Track in New Zealand, and England's Cotswold Way. Thirty-five years earlier, he'd even wandered into my all-time favorite Irish pub, Nancy's, in Ardara, County Donegal.

Patrick recommended many more destinations I'd yet to visit. I jotted them down on a cardboard beer coaster.

"When you get to these places, be sure to look at the day," he said.

I glanced up at him. "Look at the day?"

"Look at the day."

"What do you mean?"

His eyes twinkled. "Just look at the day."

I thought for a moment. "Oh, you mean, the details are on the ground."

Patrick clapped his hands once. "Exactly."

STRAYS

Andrea took Maya and me in within days of each other. Maya was apparently abandoned in the neighborhood, and I was coming off the road after four years. Maya was housebroken, and I was trying to be.

The vet who spayed Maya estimated her age to be about six months, but he couldn't determine her breed.

"She's very unusual," he said.

Although she had a sweet disposition, Maya had a wild look about her. Coyotes roam San Diego's urban canyons, and I speculated whether Maya was a hybrid—a coydog or a dogote.

"Could be," the vet agreed, but he winked when he said this.

Now that Maya and I had a fixed address, the first thing we did was hop into Andrea's car, and the three of us left town. We crossed the border into Tijuana, and after skirting the bullring by the sea we drove south along the Pacific Coast.

San Quentín, roughly two hundred miles below San Diego, marked the farthest we'd ever ventured into Baja California. (Andrea and me, anyway. Who knew where Maya had been?) By this stage of my life, I'd traveled around the world a few times but had neglected my own backyard. Not so different from many American wanderers, I suppose.

In El Rosario we stopped for lunch at Mama Espinoza's, a legendary roadhouse that serves as a checkpoint for the annual Baja 1000 off-road race. We enjoyed their sumptuous lobster burritos. On the way out we signed the decades-old guestbook and left a little money for the orphanage that the restaurant supports.

After El Rosario the Transpeninsular Highway turned inland. Cardón cactus, barrel cactus and yucca plants sprang from the desert. Traffic and population thinned considerably. The road was narrow, but the potholes few. The backseat was heaped with camping gear. Maya dozed atop the pile, her head resting on the console between our seats.

The sun was setting when the road turned back toward the Pacific. We overnighted in Guerrero Negro, home of one of the world's largest salt works. Had it been winter we would've lingered and visited nearby Laguna Ojo de Liebre, where thousands of migrating grey whales return each year during calving season. Another trip.

The next day the highway headed east again across the desert. We stopped in San Ignacio, a palm-fringed oasis surrounded by mesas. We parked near the shady plaza and strolled through the Misíon San Ignacio Kadakaamán, dating from 1728. Maya sat in front of the carved doors and posed for her first photo.

At Santa Rosalía, we caught our first glimpse of the Sea of Cortez, which separates the Baja peninsula from the Mexican mainland. The town was founded by a French copper mining company in the nineteenth century and boasts an unusual attraction: a prefabricated iron-walled church designed by

Gustave Eiffel, architect of the Eiffel Tower. Originally built as a model for missionary churches in France's tropical colonies, the church was exhibited with Eiffel's famous tower at the 1889 Paris World Exposition. When a French mining magnate learned the church was warehoused in Belgium, he bought it and shipped it in sections to Santa Rosalía. It was reassembled there in 1897 and named Iglesia Santa Bárbara.

We exited the church, Maya in tow, and encountered a dog sitting on the dusty sidewalk in the hot sun. He was the most forlorn creature I'd ever seen. He had but a few matted clumps of hair, and his skin was dark and greasy. He sat with one leg aloft, as if it were too painful to rest all four limbs on this earth. We brought him some food and water from the car, but he ignored it. I wondered what had happened to him and if he had already given up.

"That could have been you," I said.

"Awww," Andrea said, thinking I meant Maya, but I was talking about myself.

We had no destination, but we knew where to stop. South of Mulegé we spotted a string of sandy beaches, each lovelier than the last. We pulled down a dirt track, past a sign that read, "Playa Coyote." The road delivered us to a crescent of golden sand flanking Bahía Concepción, a national marine preserve. Several small, rocky islands dotted the warm, crystal clear water. Ten or so palapas lined the beach, none of them occupied. It was early September. Schools were back in session and snowbirds had yet to arrive with their RVs. We had this paradise to ourselves; there wasn't even anyone to collect the camping fee.

We pitched our tent next to one of the open-sided huts, in the shade of three palm trees. We strung a hammock between two palapa poles and rolled out a couple beach mats. At night, we grilled the local catch on our gas barbecue and drank Bohemias by candlelight. We played Los Lobos and Louis Armstrong on the boombox and gazed at the brilliant stars above. After we went to bed, Maya barked at the beach's namesake coyotes when they wandered too close.

One night bioluminescent plankton turned the bay a dazzling green. Andrea, Maya and I waded into the water. When our legs stirred the light-emitting organisms, we were treated to a light show, as comet-like tails streaked beneath the surface of the sea.

I don't recall how long we stayed at Coyote Beach. I do know we stayed long enough for an important transformation to occur in our lives—although we had no way of knowing it at the time. Looking back after all these years, it's easy to see: we had started the journey as three individuals and ended it as a family.

THANK YOU

Thank you for reading *The Distance Between.* I'd be grateful if you'd take the time to share your opinion of it with other readers at Amazon.com and Goodreads.com, or wherever you go to discuss books.

Also, if you'd like to get an email when I publish my next book, please sign up here: http://eepurl.com/Jl_gn

Many thanks!
Mike McIntyre

ABOUT THE AUTHOR

Mike McIntyre is an author, journalist and traveler. His journeys have taken him to more than eighty countries. He has worked as a travel columnist for the *Los Angeles Times*, a theater columnist for the *Washington Post*, and a feature writer for the *San Diego Union-Tribune* and the *Budapest Sun*. He's also published articles in *Golf Digest*, *Reader's Digest*, *Air & Space/Smithsonian* and *Powder* magazines. When not traveling, he lives in San Diego.

ALSO BY MIKE MCINTYRE

The Kindness of Strangers: Penniless Across America

The #1 Amazon Travel Bestseller.

As featured on Oprah, *The Kindness of Strangers* is the story of one man's continental leap of faith—and the country that caught him.

Stuck in a job he no longer found fulfilling, journalist Mike McIntyre felt his life was quickly passing him by. So one day he hit the road to trek from one end of the country to the other with little more than the clothes on his back and without a single penny in his pocket. Through his travels, he found varying degrees of kindness in strangers from all walks of life—and discovered more about people and values and life on the road in America than he'd ever thought possible. The gifts of food and shelter he received along the way were outweighed only by the touching gifts of the heart—the willingness of many he met to welcome a lonely stranger into their homes…and the discovery that sometimes those who give the most are the ones with the least to spare.

The Wander Year: One Couple's Journey Around the World

Mike McIntyre and his longtime girlfriend, Andrea, are in their early 40s and itching for a break. So they rent out their San Diego home—dog, cat and furniture included—and embark on a yearlong journey around the world. "We're not out to find ourselves, or even to lose ourselves," McIntyre writes early on. "We're merely seeking a pause in our routines." But the couple is soon swept up in the adventure of a lifetime: trekking in the Himalayas, traversing the Sahara on camel, scrambling over the temples of Angkor, crossing the world's largest salt flat in South America, scaling a New Zealand glacier. The book recounts the odyssey in 48 dispatches from 22 countries. Among them: birdwatching in Indonesia, a haircut from Vietnam's oldest barber, touring a notorious prison in Bolivia, haggling over rugs in Morocco, on safari in Nepal. McIntyre taps his self-deprecating humor to convey the joys, perils and frustrations of prolonged travel. When the couple ventures into a cyclone in Fiji on a rubber raft, he writes, "The absence of life jackets and paddles meant more room for our lunacy." And during a ride across India with a hired car and driver, he notes, "His passing technique was so precise, I could see my horrified expression reflected in the chrome bumpers of onrushing trucks." He also writes eloquently of such poignant moments as sleeping under the stars in North Africa, flying kites with a poor boy in Bali, and the death of a female tour guide in China. By journey's end, he's shucked much of his journalist's cynicism, and he stands in awe of a staggeringly beautiful world and the resilient souls who fill it.

The Wander Year is an expanded version of the popular series of the same name that ran in the Travel section of the *Los Angeles Times*.

The Scavenger's Daughter: A Tyler West Mystery

Disgraced newsman Tyler West is desperate for a scoop that will save his career. When he investigates the baffling deaths of several of San Diego's elite, he uncovers a common link: torture devices not used since the Dark Ages. Plunged into a mysterious world of medieval torture scholars, antiquities collectors and sadomasochists, he must break the brilliantly conceived series of slayings that has cast a dark shadow over a city better known for its sun, sand and surf. The elusive killer goes by the name Friar Tom, in tribute to his hero, Tomás de Torquemada, the first Grand Inquisitor of the Spanish Inquisition. As Ty scrambles to unmask the monstrous zealot, he is drawn into a lethal game of cat and mouse that could cost him everything.

Made in the USA
San Bernardino, CA
05 December 2017